ADVANCE PRAISE

"Michael helped us raise our third fund. He was the third set of attorneys I have worked with. I will not be looking for new attorneys anymore. Michael is professional, incredibly responsive, and thoroughly knowledgeable about all things investment-related. I could not endorse him more strongly."

—GABE BODHI, FOUNDING PARTNER, TEKTON GROUP

"Michael is unquestionably the best fund attorney out there. That's obvious from the first time you meet him. What comes out as you start working together is that he's also one of the most genuinely incredible human beings, too. Scholastic wouldn't be anywhere without him."

—SEAN O'DOWD, MANAGING DIRECTOR, SCHOLASTIC CAPITAL

"Michael Huseby has the rare ability to concisely distill complex subject matters while also providing the practical application of each topic. I have been fortunate to have had Michael as my go-to resource for all things 'funds,' and I am confident that his book will similarly serve as a comprehensive—yet easily understood—guide."

—ADRIAN PINTO, FOUNDING PARTNER, CARAVEL CAPITAL

"Michael has been my lawyer for a number of years, so I have firsthand experience seeing his quality of work. He's one of the most talented fund formation lawyers with a unique skillset of taking complex terms and topics and distilling them down into user-friendly words and concepts. Having written two books for the venture capital industry myself, I know Fundamentals is both valuable and a must-read for anyone aspiring to be knowledgeable and an expert in venture capital, the art of managing a fund, or running a syndicate."

—WINTER MEAD, FOUNDER, COOLWATER CAPITAL

"Michael is an expert in all things fund formation and securities law. We've worked closely with his team and followed his Fundamentals blog since inception. Fundamentals is a must-read for emerging managers and really any individual considering raising capital through a fund, SPV or otherwise."

—SEAN SMITH, MANAGING PARTNER,
SEARCH FUND VENTURES

"If you believe Feynman's adage that 'If you really want to master something, teach it,' then you have to recognize Michael's mastery of fund formation law. He has the unique ability to break down complex topics into easily digestible pieces in an entertaining way. This book aggregates and expands upon his valuable insights that have guided countless professionals, including myself as I launched Nord Associates."

—LEIF GUNDERSON, PRINCIPAL, NORD ASSOCIATES

"When I needed investment legal counsel a year ago, Michael Huseby came highly recommended—and now I understand why. In our work together, Michael has consistently demonstrated an exceptional combination of sharp legal acumen and genuine care for our best interests. What impresses me most is how he makes complex legal matters accessible without oversimplifying them. His leadership skills are evident in how his entire team operates with the same level of professionalism and dedication. Michael stands out in a field where technical expertise is expected because he brings both brilliance and humanity to his practice. Though we've worked together for just a little over a year, I've come to consider Michael not just my lawyer, but a trusted advisor and friend. For anyone seeking investment legal counsel, I recommend Michael Huseby without hesitation. He knows the law inside and out and leverages that expertise to achieve exceptional results for his clients."

—ANTONIA BOTERO, PRINCIPAL, MADDPROJECT

"Michael Huseby is an absolute wealth of knowledge when it comes to investment law, and his meteoric rise within the industry has certainly not been surprising. I feel very fortunate to have first met Michael when he was a pivotal member of the team that helped form our real estate fund. As talented as he is as an attorney, he's an even better person—someone I feel lucky to call a friend!"

—DON TEPMAN, PRINCIPAL, TOWNCENTRE CAPITAL (A.K.A. STRIPMALLGUY)

"Fundamentals: Your Friendly Guide to Investment Funds and Syndications is a refreshingly approachable guide to the often intimidating world of capital raising. Written by securities attorney Michael Huseby of TIL, this book breaks down complex topics like fund formation, syndications, regulatory compliance, and structuring strategies into plain, practical language. Whether you're a first-time syndicator or an emerging fund manager, Fundamentals offers clear explanations, real-world tips, and useful checklists to help you navigate the modern capital-raising landscape with confidence. It's the book you wish you'd had before launching your first deal.

On a personal note, we hired TIL to handle our first fund, and they were incredible to work with. Professional, responsive, and deeply knowledgeable—they made a daunting process feel smooth and manageable. We couldn't recommend them enough."

—DANIEL MORGAN, PRINCIPAL, MARTERRA RESIDENTIAL VENTURES

FUNDAMENTALS

Fundamentals

YOUR FRIENDLY GUIDE
TO INVESTMENT FUNDS
AND SYNDICATIONS

Michael Huseby

LIONCREST
PUBLISHING

FUNDAMENTALS
Your Friendly Guide to Investment Funds and Syndications

FIRST EDITION

ISBN   978-1-5445-4876-0   *Hardcover*
       978-1-5445-4875-3   *Paperback*
       978-1-5445-4874-6   *Ebook*

Contents

Part II: How to Comply with Laws Governing Investment Funds

Introduction

What Is an Investment Fund?

This book is not a fluffy, feel-good book about how to get rich stuffed with words for the sake of words. It's a no-frills manual about how to get the job done (without going to jail).

Investment funds sound complicated (and in some ways, they are), but this book will simplify the process of forming and raising them. This process doesn't have to be confusing or stressful. I do it every day, and I'll talk to you just like I talk to my clients who are emerging managers. Let's start at the beginning.

WHAT IS AN INVESTMENT FUND?

An investment fund is a vehicle that pools money from a bunch of different investors, called limited partners (LPs). The fund's general partner (GP) runs the show, while the LPs are largely passive.

A typical investment fund invests in multiple assets across a single industry. For example, a private equity fund might focus on manufacturing businesses, a real estate fund might focus on multifamily apartments in Texas, or a venture capital fund might focus on emerging SaaS businesses.

A syndication is like a fund, but it only invests in one thing. Instead of investing in multiple businesses or properties, it holds just a single asset. Syndications are also called "SPVs" (special purpose vehicles), but we'll usually call them "syndications" in this book.

WHY DO PEOPLE FORM INVESTMENT FUNDS?

LPs like investment funds because they provide diversification and the potential for outsized investment returns. Top GPs often outperform the market, and some asset classes (like real estate) offer tax-advantaged income.

GPs like investment funds because they provide a way to (potentially) make a lot of money while solving interesting problems. As we'll discuss in Chapter 2, GPs enjoy multiple potential streams of income from funds and syndications. While being a GP comes with unique challenges and stressors, the potential upside for successful managers is massive.

WHAT WILL YOU LEARN IN THIS BOOK?

This book is split into two parts. In Part I, you'll learn how to form and raise your investment fund or syndication, including:

- How long it takes to raise a fund
- How to structure your compensation
- Who to recruit on your team
- How to choose between a multi-asset fund and a single-asset syndication
- How to choose between a closed-end and an open-end fund
- How to dictate your fund's business and legal terms

- How to distribute money to LPs
- How to prepare your fund's legal documentation
- How to negotiate with LPs
- How to formally admit LPs into your fund
- How to call capital from LPs

In Part II, you'll learn how to comply with the laws applicable to investment funds and syndications, including:

- The Securities Act
- The Investment Company Act
- The Investment Advisers Act
- State laws
- Tax laws

Each chapter has a "Fund Trap"—a quick trip to avoid disaster. These are real (anonymized) stories from the field. After reading this book, you'll know more than many GPs who have already successfully raised money (I'm not joking). If you're unsure what a word means, look it up in the glossary at the end of the book. I suspect I'll see you there more than a few times! Please note that the laws may have changed since this book was published. Always, always, always work with a qualified lawyer to ensure regulatory compliance.

WHY SHOULD YOU BELIEVE WHAT I HAVE TO SAY?

At the law firm TIL (check us out at til.law), we form funds and syndications all day. In fact, that's all I've done for years, previously at big law firms like Latham & Watkins and DLA Piper and now at TIL, a specialty shop focused exclusively on private investments.

I'm also a GP in a real estate fund, which I helped form. Getting a fund off the ground as a GP was a great experience because it gave me a first-person view into the life of a fund manager (and what it takes to be successful).

We at TIL have a newsletter at fundamentals.law that discusses funds and syndications. The newsletter is a companion to this book, and we're constantly updating the newsletter and following market trends. Join us there!

Enough about me. Let's get to the good stuff. We'll start with the question everybody asks: how long does it actually take to raise a fund?

PART I

How to Raise an Investment Fund (or Syndication)

CHAPTER 1

How Long Does It Take to Raise a Fund?

Now that you've decided to become a successful fund manager, it's time to learn how this all works. If you're in a hurry, you might be wondering, "How soon can we close?"

BUDGET AT LEAST A MONTH TO RAISE YOUR FUND

The short answer: if everything goes smoothly and LPs sign their documents quickly, GPs can go from start to finish in roughly **one month** after contacting a fund-formation lawyer.

We once completed the whole process in three weeks, but it was intense for everyone. I don't recommend it. For a comfortable pace, I would budget six weeks.

Now, let's discuss the "pre-work" you should do before contacting an attorney and officially starting your fundraise.

WHAT TO DO BEFORE TALKING TO A LAWYER

Contacting a fund-formation lawyer is one of the most crucial first steps to forming a fund (and I'm not just saying that because I'm a fund-formation lawyer). Your attorney will guide you through the whole process and quarterback your fundraise.

However, to save time (and money), you should do as much legwork as possible before contacting a lawyer. Many attorneys bill by the hour. If you come to them with a half-baked idea and don't know what you're talking about, it will cost you.

Here's a list of tasks to complete before getting a lawyer involved:

TARGET YOUR ASSET CLASS

Determine which specific asset class you want to focus on. Your target investment class will inform the entire fund-formation process. You should be an expert uniquely suited to generate strong investment returns.

Specific is usually better than general when choosing an asset class. I once saw someone try to raise a hybrid venture capital/private equity/real estate fund. Don't do that! LPs often prefer specialized funds to diversified ones—they prefer to handle the diversification themselves (by picking the best fund managers in each niche).

DECIDE WHETHER YOU WANT A MULTI-ASSET FUND OR A SINGLE-ASSET SYNDICATION

We will discuss funds versus syndications in depth in Chapter 4. But briefly, multi-asset funds invest in multiple assets, such as several different apartment buildings, software companies, or home services businesses. Single-asset syndications buy individual assets, such as one apartment building, shares in one fintech company, or one HVAC business. As discussed in Chapter 4, many new GPs start with syndications and level up to funds once they have a track record of successful investments (and happy LPs).

DECIDE WHETHER YOU WANT A
CLOSED-END OR OPEN-END FUND

We will discuss these fund types in detail in Chapter 5. In short, closed-end funds have a defined lifespan and are more common in illiquid asset classes, like real estate, private equity, and venture capital. Investors in closed-end funds typically don't achieve liquidity until the end of the fund's life. Open-end funds are more common in liquid asset classes, like public equities. These funds have no defined term (they can last forever), and investors can usually withdraw money throughout the life of the fund after a lock-up period.

RESEARCH MARKET TERMS

Try to get a sense of what the market is in your industry. You don't want to offer terms that are confusing or absurd. Ask other GPs. Ask your potential LPs (they're the ones who matter most). Your lawyer can also help with this.

DRAFT A PRELIMINARY MARKETING DECK

Your deck should include your thesis, tentative terms, and background. It should be anywhere from ten to thirty pages long, on average, preferably with charts and graphs explaining the investment opportunity and your track record. You can adjust the deck later based on feedback from your lawyer and potential investors.

REACH OUT TO FRIENDS AND FAMILY

Discuss your potential fund or syndication with people close to you. Solicit critical feedback. Ask if they want to invest with you. If your friends and family aren't interested in your idea, you may have a lackluster offering. In that case, go back to the drawing board.

COLLECT "SOFT COMMITMENTS" FROM POTENTIAL INVESTORS

Keep a list of investors who have expressed interest in your fund. After you prepare the official fund documents with your lawyer, send subscription documents to these investors so they can officially invest in your fund or syndication.

⚠ FUND TRAP #1: GOING TO A LAWYER WITH A HALF-BAKED IDEA

Take the time to research and develop your fund's terms and structure *before* going to a lawyer. Preparation is crucial. Flip-flopping and constantly changing your mind can result in confused LPs, a frustrated GP team, and a frightening legal bill.

At a large law firm where I previously worked, there was a client who changed their mind at a dizzying rate. They changed fund structures, business terms, and even the members of the GP team. An LP dropped out because of the confusion. And the legal bill was...higher than the client wanted. If you are uncertain about major aspects of your fund, as that client was, it makes sense to do your own research before contacting (and paying) a professional. Then, talk to an expert when your decisions are firm. You'll thank me later.

Now that that's out of the way, let's walk through the three major steps of the official fund-formation process.

STEP 1: PREPARE LEGAL SUMMARY OF TERMS AND MARKETING DECK

Once you have done your research, made your decisions, and completed all the necessary preparation discussed in the last section, it's time to contact everyone's favorite person—a lawyer! Your fund-formation attorney will help you draft a comprehensive summary of terms for your fund. This isn't a one-page teaser. It's serious business. A syndication's summary of terms might be four to ten pages long. A multi-asset fund's summary of terms might be fifteen to twenty pages.

We'll discuss the legal and business terms to include in this document in Chapter 6. For now, just know this summary of terms will have the vast majority of business terms your potential LPs will want to know before deciding to invest.

Once your summary of terms is complete, you can revise your marketing deck to include an updated set of terms. Your lawyer may also have some comments on your marketing deck from a securities law perspective. We'll discuss securities law in detail in Part II.

HOW LONG DOES IT TAKE TO DRAFT
A SUMMARY OF TERMS?

Drafting the summary of terms can take as little as a day or two for a straightforward fund or syndication. In some cases (such as if you have non-US or tax-exempt investors), finalizing the summary of terms might take a week or more, as tax counsel and other specialists may need to weigh in.

STEP 2: DRAFT FUND DOCUMENTS
AND FORM LEGAL ENTITIES

Once the summary of terms is finalized, your lawyer can start preparing the key long-form documents to send to investors, including the limited partnership agreement, subscription documents, and private placement memorandum. We'll discuss these documents (as well as some less exciting documents) in detail in Chapter 8.

During this step, your lawyer will also form the various legal entities in your fund structure, including the fund, the GP, and the management company. We'll discuss these entities in depth in Chapter 2.

HOW LONG DOES IT TAKE TO DRAFT
THE FUND DOCUMENTS?

Drafting fund documents might take anywhere from two to four weeks, depending on the complexity of your fund's structure. Syndication documents can often be prepared in less time because the agreements are simpler and more straightforward.

However, some cases—especially if you need to involve multiple law firms—can take longer. For example, if you have non-US investors in a real estate fund, you might need to hire a law firm in the Cayman Islands or British Virgin Islands. We'll discuss why in Chapter 16.

Forming the legal entities is usually a straightforward process and doesn't take more than a week or so.

STEP 3: SIGN THE DOCUMENTS AND HOLD AN INITIAL CLOSING

Here comes the fun part! There are two main components to getting LPs to sign the fund documents:

1. **LP Negotiations.** Your investors might want to change some of the terms in your fund documents. We'll discuss negotiation strategy and mechanics in Chapter 9.
2. **Signing the Documents.** You'll need to herd the cats and get them to sign on the dotted line. We'll discuss this process in Chapter 10.

In addition to signing documents, your lawyers will file documents with the Securities and Exchange Commission (SEC) on your behalf and otherwise ensure the fund holds a proper closing.

HOW LONG DOES IT TAKE TO SIGN THE DOCUMENTS?

In some funds, LPs are impressively on task and sign the documents promptly. However, in most funds, GPs must follow up, follow up, and follow up again! Especially during the summer, when the fanciest LPs are galivanting around France or Italy. Communication is key—let your LPs know the target initial closing date well in advance so they can be ready to sign.

Aside from getting LPs to sign, the rest of the closing mechanics (such as the securities filings) can be done relatively quickly.

Overall, this step can take anywhere from a couple of days to several months. It all depends on the LPs.

HOW TO RAISE YOUR FUND AS QUICKLY AS POSSIBLE

To raise your fund at lightning speed, follow these tips:

1. **Don't Flip Flop.** After choosing a course, stay consistent. Don't constantly change your terms and revise the structure. Changes cost precious time (and legal fees).
2. **Communicate.** Keep in constant contact with your potential LPs, informing and reminding them of the target closing date and explaining the subscription process. Don't surprise your investors. LPs hate surprises! Also, respond to your lawyer and administrator quickly so they can do their jobs as efficiently as possible.
3. **Decline/Defer Negotiations.** Investor negotiations can be time-consuming. To raise money quickly, offer LPs a "take it or leave it" deal. Whether you can pull this off successfully depends on your bargaining power.

Alright, now that you have an idea of the typical fund-formation timeline, let's get to the good stuff—how you'll get paid!

CHAPTER 2

How Will You Be Paid for Managing the Fund?

Let's discuss how investment fund managers get rich. Or, at least, how they *might* get rich.

THE TWO KEY "MANAGEMENT" ENTITIES—THE GP AND THE MANCO

Investment fund managers often have two "management" entities:

- **General Partner ("GP").** This is the legal control entity of the fund. The GP receives the carried interest earned from the fund (I explain carried interest below). The GP is often a mere holding entity (i.e., not an operating business) formed specifically for each fund. Each time you form a new fund or syndication, you form a new GP.
- **Management Company ("ManCo").** This is the overarching management business. It's an operating business that might

have employees, offices, and other trappings of an actual company. The GP often delegates management of the fund to the ManCo in exchange for the ManCo receiving the management fee (discussed below). The ManCo lasts forever, and a single ManCo can serve as the management company for all your funds and syndications.

The following chart shows the structure of a relatively simple investment fund.

Basic Fund Structure

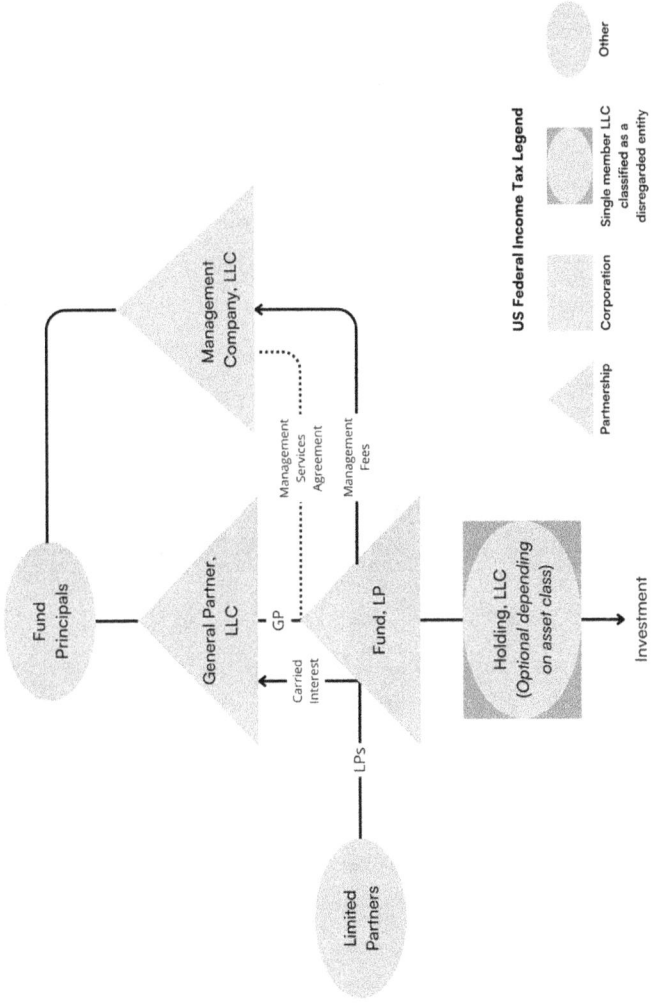

Limited Partners — LPs → Fund, LP

Fund Principals → General Partner, LLC (GP) and Management Company, LLC

General Partner, LLC — Carried Interest ← Fund, LP

Management Services Agreement / Management Fees — Management Company, LLC

Fund, LP → Holding, LLC (Optional depending on asset class) → Investment

US Federal Income Tax Legend

- Partnership
- Corporation
- Single member LLC classified as a disregarded entity
- Other

Now, let's discuss the income streams of the GP and ManCo entities.

MANAGEMENT FEES

Most funds pay the ManCo a recurring asset management fee for managing the fund. For simplicity, this is often called the "management fee" (this is *not* the same as a "property management" fee in a real estate fund, which is discussed below). The purpose of the management fee is to pay ManCo/GP expenses, which you will learn more about in Chapter 3.

HOW MUCH SHOULD THE MANAGEMENT FEE BE?

Management fees vary based on asset class and whether you have a multi-asset fund or a single-asset syndication (Chapter 4).

Let's look at some examples.

- **Venture Capital Fund:** Management fee is (i) 2 percent of committed capital during the fund's investment period and (ii) 1.5 percent of committed capital thereafter.
- **Private Equity Fund:** Management fee is (i) 2 percent of committed capital during the fund's investment period and (ii) 2 percent of invested capital thereafter.
- **Hedge Fund:** Management fee is 1.5 percent of the net asset value of the fund.
- **Real Estate Syndication:** Management fee is 2 percent of the gross revenues earned in respect of the property.

The "investment period" of a multi-asset fund is typically the first half of the fund's life (e.g., the first five years in a standard ten-year fund). We'll discuss the investment period in detail in Chapter 5.

ARE MANAGEMENT FEES A PROFIT CENTER?

In smaller funds, the fund principals (the humans running the show) are not getting rich off management fees. For example, a $15 million venture capital fund would generate management fees of $300,000 per year during the investment period and $225,000 annually thereafter (assuming their management-fee structure is the same as our example above). If there are two fund principals, that's only $150,000 per year per person (before paying outside team members, renting office space, or buying equipment), even less after the investment period ends. Not quite the poverty line but often a pay cut for people leaving cushy private equity jobs to start their own funds.

In very large funds, fees can spiral upward. For example, according to its website at the time of this writing, venture capital giant Andreessen Horowitz has $43 billion in assets under management. That's $860 million a year in asset management fees alone. Dizzying.

MANAGEMENT FEE REDUCTIONS

Some funds have "management fee offsets"—special provisions that reduce the management fee otherwise earned by the ManCo.

Examples of common management fee offsets include:

- **Placement Fees.** The ManCo team might pay third-party "placement agents" to help them raise capital. The fund will often pay for these "placement fees" initially, but the management fee will be reduced by the amount of the placement fees.
- **Excess Organizational Expenses.** Funds typically pay to set themselves up...to a point. Many funds have an "organizational expense cap." For example, if the organizational

expense cap is $150,000, and it costs $180,000 to set up the fund, the fund will pay the full $180,000, but the $30,000 excess will be deducted from the management fee otherwise earned by the ManCo.

- **Transaction Fees.** Some funds reduce the management fee by the amount paid in "transaction fees" to the ManCo or its affiliates by third parties. These fees include monitoring fees in private equity funds and board fees in venture capital funds. For example, a GP principal earns $5,000 a year for being on the board of a portfolio company, and the management fee is reduced by $5,000.

Not all funds have these management fee offsets, but they're common in mid-size and larger funds.

⚠ FUND TRAP #2: FORGOING A MANAGEMENT FEE IN A FIT OF ALTRUISM

Fund managers often think they've discovered the El Dorado of incentive alignment. Why not forego the management fee altogether? We only get paid if LPs get paid! Buffett did it.

The problem is if you have no recurring management fee, you have no way to pay ManCo employees. While this might work in the short term (or if the fund principals are independently wealthy), it doesn't work if the fund managers have a mortgage to pay.

I once had a client who wanted an entirely fee-free model. No management fees. No acquisition fees. No fees at all! In exchange for the lack of fees, the carried interest waterfall was especially rich (50 percent to the GP and 50 percent to the LPs after an 8 percent preferred return). The client had trouble fundraising. Eventually, a large prospective LP convinced the client to change to a more standard 2/20 model (2 percent management fee and 20 percent carried interest). After much hand-wringing, the client switched to 2/20 and successfully completed their fundraise.

OTHER FEES

In addition to the asset management fee, the ManCo might earn one or more of the following fees:

- **Acquisition Fees.** Fees paid when the fund buys something. For example, 1 percent of the purchase price of a business or real estate property.
- **Property Management Fees.** Fees paid to manage or monitor a property. For example, 4 percent of the gross revenue generated by an apartment building.
- **Guarantee Fees.** Fees paid to a fund principal (or an affiliate) for personally guaranteeing indebtedness. For example, 0.5 percent of the principal amount of guaranteed indebtedness.
- **Disposition Fees.** Fees paid when the fund sells something. For example, 1 percent of the gross sale price of a property.
- **Development Fee.** Fees paid for development or construction. For example, 5 percent of the hard costs of development.

There are many other potential fees, but these are the most common. Most funds won't have all the fees listed above, but, alas, some do. My personal preference is to not go overboard with fees, but I'm not the boss! Fund managers should *clearly* disclose all fees payable to the ManCo, GP, principals, or any affiliates in their marketing materials and fund documents.

CARRIED INTEREST

Carried interest is the ultimate prize. Also called "promote" or "incentive income," carried interest is the GP's share of the fund's profits.

In most funds, the GP gets somewhere around 20 to 30 percent of the fund's profits (after LPs have received a return of their initial investment capital and, potentially, a preferred return). The "distribution waterfall" is the provision that dictates the GP's carried interest rights.

For example, let's say an LP invests $100, and the fund doubles that investment to $200. How should this $200 be distributed?

In a very simple distribution waterfall:

- *First*, the LP would get $100 (a return of their capital)
- *Second*, the remaining $100 of profits would be distributed 80 percent to the LP ($80) and 20 percent to the GP ($20)

The $20 distributed to the GP is the carried interest. It's the good stuff. Unlike management fees (which are taxed as ordinary income), carried interest is often taxed at capital gains rates. At least for now. We'll walk through distribution waterfalls and carried interest in excruciating detail in Chapter 7.

RETURN ON THE GP'S CAPITAL INVESTMENT (GP COMMITMENT)

In most funds, the GP invests alongside the LPs as an investor. This might be called the "GP commitment" or the "GP co-invest." Typically, the GP's co-investment amount is exempt from paying management fees and carried interest.

Everyone has a different opinion on this, but the GP co-invest is usually somewhere between 1 and 10 percent of committed capital. In smaller funds and syndications, GPs often invest at the top of that range. Some GPs commit more. Some commit nothing.

So how does the GP co-invest work? Let's say a GP invests 5 percent of the capital in a $20 million fund. That would make the GP's commitment $1 million. If the fund returns $40 million (a 2x multiple), the GP would get 5 percent of the proceeds ($2 million), pocketing $1 million in profit.

The distribution waterfall does not typically apply to the GP because the waterfall is where the GP takes their carried interest from the LPs. As the GP doesn't pay carried interest, they receive their distributions outside the waterfall. Some funds handle this a different way, where *everyone's* capital (including the GP's) goes through the waterfall, but this is less common in institutional funds.

HOW DO GPS FUND THEIR GP COMMITMENT?

There are three main ways GPs fund their commitment to invest:

- **Cash.** This is the simplest. The GP commits cash just like an LP. When the fund calls capital, the GP sends the same percentage of their commitment as the LPs via check, wire transfer, or Dogecoin.
- **Property.** In some cases, the GP contributes property to the fund to satisfy their commitment. In a venture capital fund, this could be shares in a startup. In a real estate fund, it could be an apartment building. The property contributed must be within the fund's target asset class (i.e., something the fund would otherwise buy). You wouldn't contribute an apartment building to a public securities fund. Additionally,

GPs should be very clear about the price at which they're contributing the property. The best practice is to have a third party appraise the property. You don't want to open yourself up to LP complaints of impropriety.

- **Fee Waivers.** GPs may also forego fees (like management fees and acquisition fees) in exchange for a "profits interest" in the fund. For example, instead of taking a cash management fee of $100 a quarter, the GP could take $90 in cash and get $10 of fund equity instead. You must absolutely work with a good tax lawyer if you want to use fee waivers—they can get tricky. We'll discuss fee waivers in detail in Chapter 16.

Now that you have a good idea of how you'll get paid, let's move on to learning about who will be paid by you—your team members! A stellar team is worth the cost of building it out.

CHAPTER 3

Who Do You Need on Your Team?

Now that you understand the basics of getting paid, it's time to learn who you'll need on your team to make your investment-management business successful. Even "solo GPs" need most (or all) of the team members described below. You can't do it alone!

But first, let's discuss how you're going to pay for all this.

FUND EXPENSES—FEES AND EXPENSES PAYABLE BY FUNDS AND SYNDICATIONS

Investment-fund documents typically contain a definition of "fund expenses," which are costs payable by the fund itself (i.e., the capital contributions of the LPs and the GP). In practice, fund expenses are paid by the fund's bank account or credit card. In other words, fund expenses are *not* usually paid by the ManCo or the GP.

EXPENSES THAT ARE NOT FUND EXPENSES
(PAID USING THE MANAGEMENT FEE)

In general, the salaries of GP/ManCo personnel (including the principals and any other employees) are not fund expenses. Instead, these salaries are paid using the management fee (discussed in Chapter 2).

Other GP/ManCo expenses that are not typically fund expenses include:

- GP/ManCo offices
- GP/ManCo equipment, hardware, and software
- GP/ManCo-level accounting and tax returns

Often, the definition of "fund expenses" is negotiated. Depending on the bargaining power of the GP and the LPs, certain expenses may or may not be considered fund expenses, including:

- GP/ManCo regulatory costs (such as filing Form ADV)
- Fees to attend industry conferences
- Payments to placement agents for raising money
- Costs associated with certain types of litigation

EXPENSES THAT ARE FUND EXPENSES (PAID
USING FUND CAPITAL CONTRIBUTIONS)

As a general rule, fund-related expenses paid to third-party service providers are fund expenses. So, if you hire a third party to provide one of the services discussed in the next section (Key Team Members for Investment Funds and Syndications), the fund typically pays for it outside (in addition to) the management fee.

Other examples of fund expenses include:

- Entity-formation and registered-agent fees
- Blue Sky filing fees and other fund-related regulatory costs
- Diligence costs
- Travel expenses to find investments
- Payments for fund-level accounting and tax-return preparation
- Indemnification costs

REIMBURSING THE GP PRINCIPALS FOR FUND EXPENSES

Most fund documents permit the GP principals to be reimbursed by the fund for anything that's a proper fund expense. Reimbursement is particularly helpful for costs incurred before the fund's initial closing. For example, if the principals paid the fund-setup costs out of pocket, the fund would reimburse them at the fund's initial closing.

Some service providers (such as registered agents, lawyers, and administrators) might defer a portion of their fees until the fund's initial closing, which can help emerging managers with liquidity.

Now that we understand how fund expenses work, let's discuss who you need on your team.

KEY TEAM MEMBERS FOR INVESTMENT FUNDS AND SYNDICATIONS

Below are some key people you'll need on your team. Some are absolutely required, and others are optional. When interviewing potential candidates, consider asking about their cost structure, staffing model, and experience with private investment funds (very important). Ask friends for referrals.

INVESTMENT ANALYST (REQUIRED)

Investment funds and syndications need someone who can provide investment analysis and financial underwriting. These services are crucial to any investment business. Some funds have all their financial people in-house (in which case, such personnel would be paid using the management fee). Others work with outsourced contractors to help fill out their team. The financial model is critical. An LP might request your financial model, so you want to have something professional (and correct) to give them.

LAWYER (REQUIRED—AND DELIGHTFUL)

Lawyers are consistently everyone's favorite people (at least that's what I tell myself at night). Your lawyer will be the quarterback throughout the whole fund-formation process, managing several crucial aspects of building your fund, including the following:

- Choosing the business and legal terms of your fund/syndication (Chapter 6)
- Drafting fund documents (Chapter 8)
- Forming legal entities (Chapter 8)
- Negotiating with investors (Chapter 9)
- Handling securities filings with the SEC (Chapter 10)

After your fund or syndication is formed, your lawyer should stick around to help with any questions or projects you might have while running the fund. Ongoing maintenance items could include:

- LP transfers (an LP wants to sell their interest)
- LP consents (the GP needs LP approval to do something)

- Subsequent closings (see Chapter 5)
- General fund-related questions and regulatory matters

CPA (REQUIRED)

Taxes can get complicated quickly for funds and syndications. You'll need a good certified public accountant (CPA) to help prepare the fund's tax returns and issue K-1s to LPs. When interviewing CPAs, ask about their track records for getting K-1s out on time. LPs don't love receiving their tax forms in August.

Your CPA can also help with special tax structuring if you have non-US LPs, non-US investments, or tax-exempt LPs. This is especially relevant for real estate funds and syndications.

AUDITOR (REQUIRED—SOMETIMES)

Many investment funds have their annual financial statements audited. Some investment funds are legally required to have an annual audit (check out Chapters 14 and 15). Other funds do not need to engage an auditor. Ask your lawyer!

Even if an audit isn't legally required, larger funds with sophisticated LPs often have their annual financials audited regardless. If you're raising more than $50 million (or perhaps even less), LPs may demand an audit.

COMPLIANCE OFFICER (REQUIRED—SOMETIMES)

Many funds employ someone dedicated to compliance matters. This is especially true for private equity funds, hedge funds, and credit funds that are registered investment advisers (RIAs). Ask your lawyer whether you're legally required to have a chief compliance officer—it depends on your fund type and total assets under management. We'll discuss the regulatory landscape in detail in Part II.

As a general rule:

- **Most Regulated:** Private equity, private credit, hedge funds
- **Medium Regulated:** Venture capital
- **Least Regulated:** Real estate

Some funds and syndications opt to work with an outsourced compliance consultant to help them comply with the Investment Advisers Act and file/update Form ADV, a required disclosure document for RIAs (we'll discuss this further in Chapters 14 and 15). These consultants are often less expensive than an attorney (but not always).

⚠ FUND TRAP #3: TRYING TO DO IT ALL YOURSELF

Raising an investment fund or syndication is not something you can do alone. Some emerging managers try to cut costs by doing fund administration, compliance, and (gasp!) legal work themselves. This is a well-trodden road to disaster.

Our firm once had a potential client who tried to draft the fund documents themselves. Evidently, they thought using an online form limited liability company (LLC) agreement would do the trick. Ultimately, the fund documents lacked *all* the key terms we'll discuss in Chapter 6. They also handled compliance themselves and were running afoul of a state investment-advisers law.

They came to us to "fix" their fund, but we declined to engage. At a certain point, a situation can become so radioactive it is nearly impossible to remedy.

FUND ADMINISTRATOR (OPTIONAL)

A fund administrator will make your life a lot easier. They help handle the day-to-day back-office work of running a fund or syndication, including:

- Onboarding investors
- Keeping books and records
- Issuing capital calls (getting money from LPs)
- Making distributions (sending money to LPs)
- Handling expense reimbursements
- Coordinating with auditors and other service providers
- Serving as the third-party "referee" between the GP and the LPs

While not legally required, I recommend working with a good fund administrator once your budget supports it. It's a fund expense!

DESIGNER (OPTIONAL)

Many investment firms enlist a designer to make their websites and marketing decks beautiful. In some cases, the designer might also help with the private placement memorandum (PPM), creating delightful graphics and charts.

FUNDRAISER (OPTIONAL—BE CAREFUL!)

Funds need to raise money!

GP principals are often heavily involved in fundraising, but they might also hire dedicated investor-relations and fundraising personnel to add fundraising firepower. Some funds work with a placement agent to help raise money. A placement agent is a

Financial Industry Regulatory Authority (FINRA)-registered broker-dealer who typically earns a commission for raising capital.

If you are paying someone to help you raise money and compensation is conditioned on successful fundraising ("success fees"), ensure the fundraiser is a registered broker-dealer. Otherwise, both you and the fundraiser may be subject to penalties.

INSURANCE AGENT (OPTIONAL)

Funds need all kinds of insurance, and a dedicated insurance agent can be helpful. In addition to insurance specific to your asset class (e.g., liability insurance, representation and warranty insurance, flood insurance), you might also consider purchasing directors and officers (D&O) insurance. D&O insurance protects the fund's principals if they are sued for fund-related matters. Most fund documents indemnify the GP for lawsuits related to the fund (in the absence of fraud or gross negligence), but having a second layer of protection is never a bad idea.

Now that you have a sense of who you need on your team, it's time to get serious about fund structures. The first branch on the decision tree is crucial—do you want to raise a multi-asset fund or invest deal by deal with syndications?

CHAPTER 4

Do You Want a Multi-Asset "Fund" or Deal-by-Deal "Syndications"?

Now that you have a general overview of what you'll need to raise a fund or syndication, it's time to get into the nitty gritty. Beginning with this chapter, we're going to zoom in on the key decisions you'll need to make as a fund manager. The first fork in the road is whether you want to form a multi-asset fund or a single-asset syndication.

Multi-asset funds invest in more than one asset, typically over a prolonged investment period. On the other hand, single-asset syndications invest in only one asset (or a pre-packaged group of assets).

The following is a common route for aspiring GPs:

1. First, you invest your own money and see if you're any good at investing.

2. Second, you raise money from friends and family via single-asset syndications.
3. Third, after you have a few syndications under your belt, you raise a small fund. Your syndication investors often make up a large portion of your LP base.
4. Fourth, you raise a bigger fund that adds family offices and other institutions to your existing LP base of family and friends.

Obviously, everyone is different. Some people decide to stop at Step 2 or Step 3. Many people stop at Step 1 when they realize investing won't be their life's work.

If you're not sure whether to start with a fund or a syndication, this is the chapter for you.

SINGLE-ASSET SYNDICATIONS

Investment managers raise syndications when they want to invest in one thing. Examples include:

- Buying an apartment building
- Buying an HVAC company
- Investing in the Series B round of a technology company
- Loaning a tranche of debt to a single real estate development project

ADVANTAGES OF SYNDICATIONS

In many ways, raising "deal by deal" is better (and easier) than raising a fund. Let's look at some of those ways.

1. It's Easier to Raise Money with a Syndication

When you raise money for a syndication, potential investors can tangibly understand what they're investing in, and they can perform their own diligence on the asset.

For example, if you're buying an apartment complex, potential LPs can review information about the property and determine for themselves whether they agree with your underwriting. They can review financials, images, and even (theoretically) visit the property.

In another example, potential LPs in a syndication to purchase shares in a startup's Series B round can review the company's information. They can visit the company's website and try out the business's products and services for themselves.

The ability of investors to perform their own investigations makes fundraising easier. LPs can determine for themselves how they feel about the specific asset they're considering investing in, requiring less trust in the GP.

2. It's Less Expensive (and Simpler) to Raise a Syndication

Syndications are less complex than funds. As a result, they're easier to set up. To illustrate, our standard limited partnership agreement (LPA) for a simple real estate syndication is around thirty-five to forty pages long. On the other hand, the LPA for a middle-of-the-road real estate fund is eighty to one hundred pages.

Admitting investors is also usually (but not always) simpler in syndications. In funds, it's common to admit investors over a one-to-two-year period, called the "fundraising period," and deploy the capital over a three-to-five-year period, called the "investment period" (we'll discuss the lifespan of a closed-end multi-asset fund in Chapter 5). Conversely, syndications often (but not always!) raise all the money at once and deploy it immediately.

Overall, syndications generally require less work than funds (from you, your lawyers, and your accountants), which saves money, time, and mental bandwidth.

3. Syndications Have Separate Distribution Waterfalls

In most syndications, distributions of cash go something like this:

- First, LPs get their money back
- Second, LPs get a preferred return (in some asset classes)
- Thereafter, the remaining profits are split between the LPs and the GP

(Skip to Chapter 7 for a detailed walkthrough of distribution waterfalls, but only after you've had your coffee.)

Let's walk through an example:

- GP raises three syndications, each of which buys one strip mall
- Each syndication invests $100 (all LP capital; no GP capital)
- Each syndication lasts five years

Two syndications are total losses, and the third syndication has a 3x return ($300 to distribute). The GP would receive no carried interest from each of the two syndications with a total loss.

However, for the third syndication (with the 3x return), the GP would earn profits after the $100 LP investment is returned and the preferred return (let's say $40—a simple 8 percent for five years) is paid.

The remaining $160 ($300 *minus* $100 return of capital *minus* $40 preferred return) would be distributed between the LPs and the GP. In a common waterfall, the GP would get $32 (20 percent) and the LPs would get $128 (80 percent). As you'll see below, the result is much different if all three assets were bought in the same multi-asset fund. Stay tuned.

DISADVANTAGES OF SYNDICATIONS

Alas, there's no free lunch. Let's review the downsides of investing deal by deal.

1. You Fundraise 363 Days of the Year (on the Low End)

Few GPs want to spend their whole lives fundraising. They want to find deals and manage assets! If you form a new vehicle each time you find a deal, you have to raise money over and over and over again. Suddenly, you're a professional fundraiser instead of a professional investor.

Not only is constant fundraising not fun, but it can also be risky! You might assume your loyal cohort of LPs will re-up each deal, but that's only true until it's not. After investing in your first two syndications, one of your major LPs might suddenly have "liquidity issues." Trying to find that last $2 million of allocation is rarely a delightful task.

2. You Can't Deploy Capital as Quickly as Funds Can

If you need to raise money each time you put a deal together, you can't act with lightning speed. You may have found a killer asset, but now you must:

- Call your lawyer to get documents going
- Draft new marketing materials
- Call your previous investors to gauge interest
- Get everyone to sign everything and wire the money ASAP

It's certainly doable, but it takes time (and adds stress). As we'll see below, funds can act much more quickly.

3. Mo' Syndications, Mo' Problems

While forming a single syndication is easier and faster than forming a single fund, maintaining multiple single-asset syndications can get complicated quickly. Instead of having one LLC (or limited partnership) holding investor funds, you might have eight separate syndications, each with its own legal documents, bank accounts, tax returns, investors, etc. In short, you might end up in a state of chaos, wading waist-deep in a swamp of formation certificates, K-1s, and investor lists.

MULTI-ASSET FUNDS

With a fund, you form a single entity (typically a limited partnership or LLC) to invest in multiple deals over time. Common examples include:

- A private equity fund investing in small- and medium-sized businesses
- A venture capital fund investing in early-stage software companies
- A real estate fund investing in multifamily buildings in Texas
- A credit fund loaning to development projects in California

ADVANTAGES OF FUNDS

Funds can have multiple advantages over syndications. Let's explore the upsides of funds.

1. You Fundraise Once...and Then, You're Done

When you build a fund, you fundraise once. Once you've closed the fund, you can focus on acquiring, managing, and selling investments. You'll eventually need to raise the next fund, but that's often years (instead of months) in the future.

Fundraising is a grind. Anything you can do to decrease the percentage of your day spent begging people for money increases your quality of life. You can also avoid calling your lawyer as much, as you won't need to set up new entities and draft documents for each deal. (However, many investment managers absolutely love their lawyers and would view this reduction in interaction as a clear negative.)

2. You Can Act with Lightning Speed

As a fund manager, when you find a deal, you can buy it immediately. No need to organize documents and get your ducks in a row.

Fund documents typically give LPs ten business days to send money after the GP calls capital to make an investment (we'll discuss capital calls in detail in Chapter 11)—this is much faster than the time needed to form and close an entire syndication.

Moreover, some funds use "capital call facilities" to make investments. These are revolving credit facilities where funds can borrow money (using the right to call capital from LPs as collateral). If a fund has a capital call facility, it can get cash from a bank quickly, make the investment, and then pay back the loan when the capital contributions from the LPs arrive.

Obviously, not every timeline will be this fast (and GPs need time to do their diligence on each investment), but the ability to act fast is a huge benefit of funds.

3. Fewer Entities to Manage

This is mentioned in the third disadvantage of syndications, above. Making all investments through the same fund can reduce operational complexity and keep your life just a little bit simpler.

DISADVANTAGES OF FUNDS

Funds aren't for everyone. Let's consider the drawbacks to forming a fund.

1. Netted Waterfalls May Decrease GP Compensation

Let's revisit the example in the third listed advantage of syndications (Syndications Have Separate Distribution Waterfalls), above.

In a typical multi-asset fund, the returns of various deals are netted (crossed). In other words, distributions to investors might look something like this:

- First, LPs get their money back from *all* deals invested in by the fund
- Second, LPs get a preferred return (in some asset classes)
- Thereafter, the remaining profits are split between the LPs and the GP

In the example discussed in the third advantage of syndications, above, there are three investments of $100 each. If all three investments were made in the same fund, the $300 the fund has available to distribute would go 100 percent to LPs because Step 1 of the waterfall requires a return of all investor capital ($100 × 3 = $300).

So, with the exact same deals, the GP managing three separate syndications receives $32 from carried interest, while the GP managing one fund makes $0. Not fun for the GP. The LPs will be happier though!

One important note is that not all investment funds have netted (crossed) distribution waterfalls—also known as "European" waterfalls. Some funds have deal-by-deal waterfalls—also known as "American" waterfalls. In Chapter 7, we'll learn about European and American waterfalls in detail.

2. Harder to Raise Money

This is mentioned in the first listed advantage of syndications, above. Funds are "blind pooled" vehicles, which means investors pool their money with the GP but don't know the exact assets the fund will buy. It's a "trust me" approach to investing.

If LPs know and trust the GP—or the GP has a track record of success—this might not be a problem for fundraising. However, emerging managers often don't have the reputation to raise a blind-pooled, multi-asset fund right out the gate. To establish a track record and credibility, many emerging managers start out doing deal-by-deal syndications and raise a multi-asset fund only after they've proven their investing acumen.

3. Pressure to Deploy Capital at All Costs

As mentioned above, nobody knows the exact investments a typical multi-asset fund will make over its life. The actual investments will depend on market conditions, pricing, and opportunities.

But what if a venture capital fund raises $100 million to invest in Series A rounds of startups, but there aren't any good deals out there? What if all the investment opportunities are overvalued trash?

Despite their best intentions, the GP may feel compelled to invest the $100 million into companies regardless of the quality of the deals. It's unusual (though not unheard of) for a fund to leave a large portion of its capital uninvested. As a result, the caliber of a fund's investments may be lower than if the GP invested on a deal-by-deal basis and only when screaming deals were available.

⚠ FUND TRAP #4: THINKING SYNDICATIONS AREN'T SUBJECT TO THE SAME LAWS AS FUNDS

The laws we'll discuss in Part II apply to single-asset syndications as well as multi-asset funds. If you're pooling capital to make investments—even an investment in just one asset—you must comply with a host of laws and regulations. This comes as an unwelcome surprise to many syndicators.

As we'll discuss in Chapter 14, advisers to venture capital funds enjoy a special exemption from registering as an RIA under the Investment Advisers Act. However, fund managers can only use this exemption if *all* their managed funds and syndications are venture capital funds (as defined in the Investment Advisers Act).

A client once came to my firm ready to raise their first multi-asset venture capital fund, and they wanted to use the venture capital exemption to the Investment Advisers Act. However, they had previously syndicated a large number of startup investments, and some of these syndications were formed to purchase "secondary" shares (bought from another investor instead of acquired directly from the company).

Unfortunately, under the Investment Advisers Act, a manager cannot use the venture capital exemption if they have any funds or syndications that are not venture capital funds. Under the law, a syndication to purchase secondary shares is *not* a venture capital fund (much to the chagrin of managers in the venture capital industry). As a result, the GP had blown their venture capital exemption.

To fix the problem, they were forced to sell or otherwise transfer all their secondaries syndications to other GPs so they could take advantage of the venture capital exemption. Not what they had in mind when they formed those secondaries syndications!

NOTE ON RAISING MONEY FROM FAMILY AND FRIENDS

Many GPs start by raising capital from their friends and family. If you've impressed these people over the course of a long relationship, that's a good sign. The opposite is also crucial to acknowledge.

If you can't raise money from even your family and closest friends, your potential deal (or fund) probably isn't very compelling (and Thanksgiving is about to get a little more awkward). You may want to refine your pitch before reaching out to potential investors outside your inner circle.

Now that you know the difference between single-asset syndications and multi-asset funds, you can decide which one you want to build. If you choose to form a fund, your next step will be deciding whether to form a closed-end fund or an open-end fund. Turn the page to continue your adventure! If you instead want to raise money in deal-by-deal syndications for now, you can skip to Chapter 6.

CHAPTER 5

Do You Want a "Closed-End" Fund or an Evergreen "Open-End" Fund?

In Chapter 4, we compared single-asset syndications and multi-asset funds. If you've 100 percent decided you want to syndicate deal by deal, you can skip this chapter. However, if you want to be a fund manager (or aren't sure one way or the other yet), this chapter is important.

Here, we'll discuss closed-end and open-end investment funds and how they differ and then walk through the full life-cycle of a typical closed-end fund. We won't walk through the life of an open-end fund because—as you'll learn—open-end funds have a perpetual duration without distinct phases.

CLOSED-END INVESTMENT FUNDS

Let's discuss the key features of a typical closed-end fund.

1. DEFINED FUNDRAISING PERIOD

In closed-end funds, you generally have twelve to eighteen months (or longer if approved by LPs) to continue raising capital after the fund's initial closing date (the day you admit your first investors). When that period ends, the fund's "final closing date" occurs, and the fund can't accept new investors. As of the final closing date, the die is cast. No more fundraising (thank goodness).

2. DEFINED INVESTMENT PERIOD

Closed-end funds usually have an "investment period" when the fund makes investments in new assets. The investment period is typically the first half of a fund's life. After the investment period has ended, the fund can still call capital for limited purposes, such as:

- Paying fund expenses (including repaying debt)
- Follow-on investments in existing companies
- Repairs or improvements to existing properties
- Exercising options or warrants the fund already holds
- Investments that were in process as of the end of the investment period
- Investments specifically approved by the LPs

In addition, a few other things typically happen when a closed-end fund's investment period ends. For example, the management fee is normally reduced (see Chapter 2), the GP can usually start the next fund (often called a "successor fund"), and the GP's "time commitment" requirement typically decreases (usually from spending "substantially all" of their time on the fund to remaining "actively involved").

3. DEFINED FUND TERM

Closed-end funds usually have a set life. Many funds last ten years. Typically, the GP can extend the fund's life for a year or two, and the LPs can agree to further extend the fund's life.

In some funds, the LPs can terminate the fund early. The following are example provisions for terminating a fund:

- 80 percent of the LPs can end the fund's life for any reason
- 51 percent of the LPs can end the fund's life if the GP commits a "bad act" (such as fraud or gross negligence)

These LP termination rights are often negotiated by LPs and the GP.

4. LPS CAN'T WITHDRAW THEIR MONEY

In a closed-end fund, the LPs are locked in! Subject to narrow exceptions (or the good graces of the GP), investors aren't allowed to withdraw money. They get their money back over time as the fund (hopefully) makes distributions or when the fund sells its assets and distributes cash at the end of its life.

5. FUND ECONOMICS ARE "DISTRIBUTION-BASED"

This is a technical point, but economics like carried interest are based on "distributions" instead of capital account appreciation. For example, a profit split might look like this:

- First, LPs get their money back
- Second, LPs get a preferred return
- Thereafter, the GP gets 20 percent and LPs get 80 percent

The GP's right to carried interest is based on realized transactions (e.g., sales/refinances or cash flow). If the value of the fund's assets rises but nothing else happens (such as a sale or refinance), the GP would *not* typically earn carried interest in a closed-end fund.

OPEN-END INVESTMENT FUNDS

Open-end funds are an entirely different beast. Let's look at their key features and how they differ from closed-end funds.

1. UNLIMITED FUNDRAISING PERIOD

Unlike closed-end funds, open-end funds can fundraise forever. New investors are often admitted monthly or quarterly, and they contribute money into their capital accounts.

If the fund has units (shares of equity), it will have a mechanism for determining how many units an investor gets upon contributing capital.

For example, a fund may determine the price per unit by dividing the fund's net asset value by the number of units. When a new LP joins (or an existing LP increases its investment), it receives the number of units determined by dividing its capital contribution by the current price per unit.

Other funds are not "unitized"—in these funds, LPs merely get an increase in their capital account when they contribute additional funds.

2. NO INVESTMENT PERIOD

Open-end funds don't usually have an investment period. They can make investments in new businesses, products, or properties whenever they want.

3. UNLIMITED FUND TERM

Open-end funds typically have no set term. They can live forever (in theory).

4. LPS CAN WITHDRAW THEIR MONEY

If an open-end fund lasts forever, how do LPs get their money back? In open-end funds, LPs can usually withdraw their money, subject to the restrictions discussed below.

Lockup Periods

Open-end funds often have a lockup period during which LPs are not allowed to withdraw their money. In a hedge fund (or any other fund with highly liquid assets), the lockup period might be a year or two. In an illiquid asset class, like real estate or private equity, the lockup period might be much longer (two to five years or more).

If you're buying illiquid assets, you don't want people to withdraw immediately. It might be hard to raise the cash to redeem the withdrawing investors without fire-selling the fund's assets and harming the remaining LPs.

Many funds have a separate lockup period for each capital contribution an LP makes. So, if an LP puts in $100 on January 1, 2025, and $200 on January 1, 2026, those two investments would have different lockup periods.

Gates

Once the lockup period ends, LPs can start withdrawing money. However, most open-end funds also have a gate, which limits the amount of withdrawals. There are two main types of gates:

- **Fund-Wide Gates.** For example, no more than 20 percent of the fund's assets can be withdrawn in any calendar year.
- **Investor-by-Investor Gates.** For example, an LP may not withdraw more than 25 percent of its capital account in any single quarter.

Typically, any outstanding withdrawal requests (if the gate stops any withdrawals) are rolled to the next withdrawal date. As with lockup periods, illiquid asset classes tend to have stricter gates (meaning investors are subject to lower withdrawal thresholds).

5. FUND ECONOMICS ARE OFTEN "CAPITAL ACCOUNT–BASED"

In many open-end funds, the GP's carried interest is based on an LP's capital account, not distributions. What does that mean in plain English?

If a fund holds shares of Apple at $100 and the shares increase to $150, the GP can take carried interest even if the fund doesn't sell the Apple shares (and the fund makes no distributions). The capital accounts increase alongside Apple's appreciation, and that's enough for the GP to receive an incentive allocation of carried interest.

In some cases, open-end funds might be distribution-based. Distribution-based economics may be more suitable for illiquid asset classes (like real estate), where valuing the underlying investments isn't as simple as it is for assets like public equities.

⚠ FUND TRAP #5: MISMANAGING LIQUIDITY IN OPEN-END FUNDS

Open-end funds are becoming more popular than Taylor Swift (and sing at least as well—just kidding; please don't yell at me). Increasingly, GPs in private equity and real estate want the flexibility to hold high-quality assets for the long term without needing to sell.

While this can be a successful strategy, GPs seeking to raise open-end funds in illiquid asset classes should work with their attorney to craft appropriate lockup periods and gates to prevent a liquidity crunch in the event LPs start wanting to withdraw.

While a one-year lockup period and 25 percent quarterly gate might work for a hedge fund, an open-end real estate or private equity fund might want to consider significantly more restrictive lockup periods and gates. Otherwise, the fund might have to sell assets at discounted prices to meet LP redemption requests (due to the inherent illiquidity of the underlying assets).

Funds really do enforce these limits. Famously, the Blackstone REIT (dubbed BREIT) imposed withdrawal restrictions on its investors for over a year starting in November 2022. Even the big players need help managing liquidity!

WHAT'S BETTER: CLOSED-END OR OPEN-END?

Neither is inherently good or bad, better or worse. However, industry standards are as follows:

- Private equity funds are usually closed-end
- Venture capital funds are usually closed-end
- Real estate funds are usually closed-end, but some asset classes (especially buy-and-hold cash-flow strategies) may be open-end

- Debt funds may be closed-end or open-end
- Public equities funds are usually open-end

In summary:

- Illiquid strategies are usually closed-end
- Liquid strategies are usually open-end

If you want an open-end fund with an illiquid strategy, you may want to impose strict lockup periods and gates.

FULL LIFECYCLE OF A CLOSED-END INVESTMENT FUND

Now that we understand the difference between closed-end and open-end funds, let's learn the six critical phases of a closed-end fund's life.

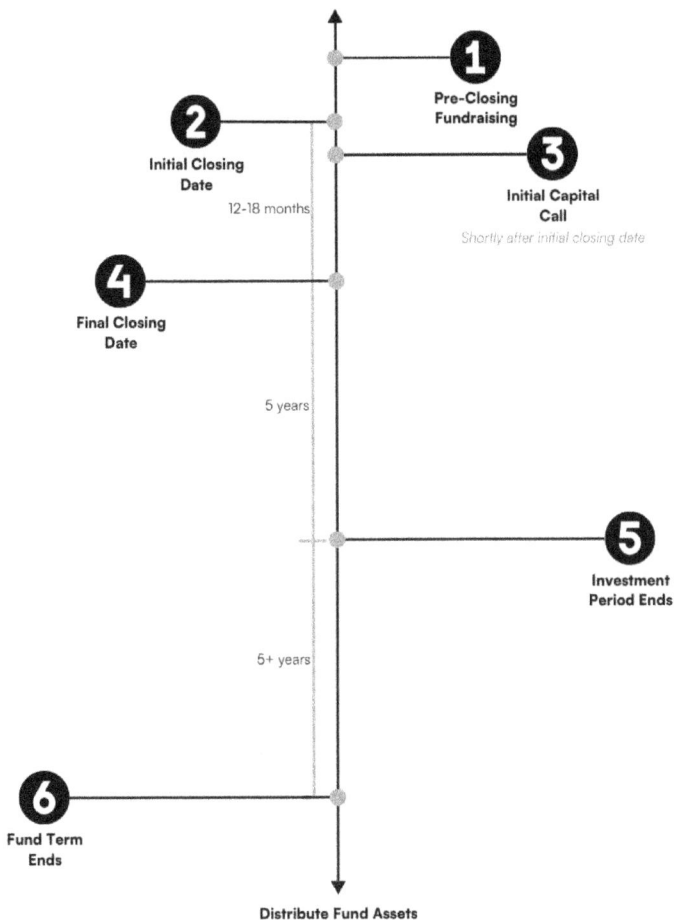

Pre-Closing Fundraising (1)

Initial Closing Date (2)

12-18 months

Initial Capital Call (3)
Shortly after initial closing date

Final Closing Date (4)

5 years

Investment Period Ends (5)

5+ years

Fund Term Ends (6)

Distribute Fund Assets

1. PRE-CLOSING FUNDRAISING

This is summarized in Chapter 1. You work with your lawyer to get your fund documents prepared and then send them to potential LPs. Chapter 12 explains who you're allowed to solicit for investment.

2. INITIAL CLOSING DATE

The initial closing date is a big deal for an investment fund. It's the day you counter-sign subscription documents and admit the first LPs. The mechanics of the initial closing are discussed in Chapter 10.

3. INITIAL CAPITAL CALL

Show me the money! Once the fund holds an initial closing, you can officially call capital from the LPs. Calling capital involves the GP sending a notice to the LPs asking for money. We'll discuss capital calls in detail in Chapter 11.

4. FINAL CLOSING DATE

Most investment funds don't raise their full target fund size at the initial closing. For example, an investment fund may have a $100 million target fund size but only close on $30 million of commitments at the initial closing. Then, it raises the remaining $70 million over the next year or two.

Most closed-end funds have a cutoff date for when fundraising must stop. A typical fundraising period lasts twelve months from the initial closing date with an optional six-month extension at the GP's discretion. This cutoff can typically be further extended if the LPs agree.

Until the final closing date, GPs often invest and fundraise simultaneously. While this is a lot of work, it enables the fund to show potential LPs a track record of actual investments, which may aid in fundraising.

5. INVESTMENT PERIOD ENDS

As discussed earlier in this chapter, closed-end funds typically have an investment period during which the fund can make new investments. The investment period is usually half the fund's life (e.g., five years in a standard ten-year fund). As discussed in Chapter 2, the management fee earned by the GP/ManCo typically decreases at the end of the investment period.

6. FUND TERM ENDS

All good things must come to an end. Eventually, the fund's term expires, at which point the fund liquidates, sells off any remaining investments, and distributes the cash to the LPs and the GP pursuant to the fund's distribution waterfall.

In some cases, the GP (and some LPs) might not want to sell the assets. The assets are great! If so, the GP may form a continuation fund to purchase the best assets from the terminating fund. In many cases, LPs can elect to tag along and keep the party going. The continuation fund might also accept new investors who weren't in the original fund.

Once you decide whether to have an open-end fund or a closed-end fund, you need to get specific. In the next chapter, you'll learn how to build out a fulsome term sheet for your fund.

CHAPTER 6

What Key Investment Terms Do You Need in Your Investment Fund or Syndication?

Once you decide on your fund's basic structure, it's time to zoom in and finalize the details. In this chapter, we'll discuss twenty key business terms you'll need to research, consider, and select for your fund or syndication.

1. CARRIED INTEREST

Carried interest is the share of the fund's profits the GP gets to keep. The LPA's distribution waterfall determines how the GP and the LPs split the money. Unlike the management fee (discussed below), carried interest is not guaranteed, and the GP may end up earning no carried interest if the fund isn't profitable. We'll discuss carried interest and distribution waterfalls in detail in Chapter 7 (you're almost there).

2. MANAGEMENT FEES

The management fee is a recurring fee paid by the fund. Typically, the management fee is paid to the ManCo pursuant to a management-services agreement entered into by the fund, the GP, and the ManCo. Management fees have two main components:

- **Management Fee Percentage:** The percentage charged.
- **Management Fee Base:** The "base" on which the management fee percentage is charged.

The typical management fee percentage and base differ based on the fund's asset class. For example, the following are common management fee bases:

- **Closed-End Venture Capital Fund:** Committed capital
- **Closed-End Real Estate or Private Equity Fund:** Committed capital during the investment period; invested capital thereafter
- **Closed-End Private Credit Fund:** Invested capital
- **Open-End Fund:** Net asset value or assets under management

In most funds, there is a reduction in the management fee when the investment period ends. We touched on this in Chapter 2.

In a private equity fund, for example, the management fee base decreases (as shown above). So, the management fee might be (i) 2 percent of committed capital during the investment period, and (ii) 2 percent of invested capital thereafter.

In a venture capital fund, however, the management fee base typically stays the same (committed capital), but the management fee percentage decreases. For example, the management fee might be (i) 2 percent of committed capital during the investment period, and (ii) 1.5 percent of committed capital thereafter.

3. OTHER AFFILIATED FEES

The fund documents should clearly and carefully disclose any other fees paid to the GP, the ManCo, or their affiliates. As discussed in Chapter 2, examples of common fees (with typical ranges) include:

- Acquisition fees (1–2 percent of gross acquisition price)
- Guarantee fees (0.5–1 percent of guaranteed indebtedness)
- Disposition fees (1 percent of gross sales price)
- Property management fees (3–7 percent of rents)
- Development fees (5 percent of the costs of development)

The ranges above are merely examples. You may see higher or lower fees in the wild. Real estate funds normally have one or more of the above fees, while other types of funds, such as venture capital funds, usually do not have any of them.

4. FUND TERM

The fund term is how long the fund lasts. A closed-end fund might last ten years, while an open-end fund could last forever. See Chapter 5 for an in-depth review of typical fund terms.

5. INVESTMENT PERIOD

The investment period is the period during which a closed-end fund can make new investments. It's typically the first half of the fund term. See Chapter 5 for an in-depth review of a typical fund investment period.

6. SUBSEQUENT CLOSINGS

How will new LPs be admitted after the initial closing date? As discussed in Chapter 5, most closed-end funds have a final closing date after which no new LPs can join.

Many closed-end funds require LPs admitted after the initial closing date to pay late fees. These late fees are paid to the early LPs to compensate them for taking the risk earlier (and to recognize the time value of money). We'll discuss the mechanics of admitting LPs after the initial closing date in detail in Chapter 11.

7. FUND EXPENSES

Fund expenses are costs paid directly by the fund (i.e., the LPs and the GP to the extent of their own capital commitment). We discussed fund expenses in detail in Chapter 2.

8. GP COMMITMENT

How much money is the GP putting into the fund? The bare minimum is typically 1 percent of the fund size, but many GPs put in much more. Occasionally, you'll see a fund or syndication where the GP has no capital commitment. Unsurprisingly, LPs prefer larger GP commitments. As discussed in Chapter 2, GPs can get creative in how they fund their commitment, including cash contributions, property contributions, and waivers of fees (like management fees or acquisition fees).

9. GP REMOVAL

Can the LPs remove the GP? Sometimes. Here are the two primary options:

- **Removal for Cause:** Many funds give LPs the right to remove the GP if the GP commits a "cause event" (something really bad, like fraud or material violation of securities laws). The required LP vote to remove for cause might be anywhere from 51 to 66 percent.
- **Removal for Any Reason:** A smaller number of funds let the LPs kick out the GP for any reason. The required LP vote to remove for any reason is often higher, perhaps 66–85 percent. In addition, for "no cause" removal, the right to remove might only begin a year or two after the fund starts. That way, the LPs can't kick out the GP without giving the GP a fair chance to perform.

As you can imagine, the definition of "cause" is highly negotiated, with GPs wanting a narrower version of "cause" and LPs negotiating a broader set of events (such as gross negligence) that can be considered a cause event.

10. KEY PERSON EVENT

Many funds require the "key persons" (the individuals running the fund) to dedicate a certain amount of time to the fund. Examples of key-person time commitments include:

- Substantially all of their business time
- A majority of their business time
- A substantial amount of their business time
- Remain "actively involved" in the affairs of the fund

If the required threshold of key persons (such as a majority) fails to uphold their time-commitment requirement, the fund often enters a "suspension period" during which the fund can't make any new investments until the LPs vote to end the suspension period. It's similar to the investment period ending.

11. INVESTMENT LIMITATIONS

Some funds have contractual limitations on what the fund can invest in or how much can be invested in a particular category. Examples of fund-wide investment limitations include:

- No more than 20 percent of commitments can be invested in a single investment
- No more than 20 percent of commitments can be invested outside the United States
- At least 75 percent of commitments must be invested in multifamily buildings in Utah
- No investments in public securities
- No investments outside North America

The LPs (or the LPAC—see #18, below) can typically waive these limitations under certain circumstances. In some cases, LPs might have their own unique investment restrictions in a side letter with the fund. If the fund were to make one of these excluded investments, the LP with the side letter would not participate in that investment. We'll discuss side letters in Chapter 9.

12. LEVERAGE

Some funds have contractual limitations on how much debt the fund can incur. For example, a multifamily real estate fund might limit leverage to 50 percent of the total value of its assets.

As discussed in Chapter 14, venture capital funds should limit their total indebtedness to 15 percent of the fund size to ensure they maintain a good "venture capital exemption" from the Investment Advisers Act. In practice, most venture capital funds don't take on any debt (except potentially short-term "capital call facilities," which enable the fund to draw down capital from a credit facility and repay the debt with capital called from LPs).

13. CO-INVESTMENTS

In some funds, LPs are given pro rata rights to invest in co-investments or follow-on investments with respect to the fund's portfolio investments (or, potentially, outside investments).

For example, let's say a fund invests in the Series A round of a tech company. Later, the fund has the opportunity to invest in the Series B round, but the allocation is more than the fund can invest by itself (for example, a $40 million allocation in a $100 million fund).

In this situation, the fund might spin up a syndication to invest in the Series B round and give each fund LP the right to invest in the syndication. In many cases, fund LPs would get preferential economic rights (such as reduced fees or carried interest) in the co-investment syndication.

14. SUCCESSOR FUNDS

Most funds prohibit the GP from raising a "successor fund" (the next fund) before the investment period is over (typically halfway through the fund's life). "Successor fund" is usually narrowly defined to mean a fund substantially identical to the existing fund. For example, the principals of a private equity fund couldn't raise another private equity fund until the fund's investment period ends. However, they could raise a venture capital fund or a real estate fund.

15. LP WITHDRAWAL RIGHTS

In most closed-end funds, LPs can't withdraw money before the fund term ends. They're locked in. Open-end funds typically permit LPs to withdraw, subject to lockups (time-based restrictions) and gates (amount-based restrictions). For more on lockups and gates, see Chapter 5.

16. IN-KIND DISTRIBUTIONS

Can the fund distribute anything other than cash to the LPs? For example, restricted securities? Many funds limit "distributions in kind" (distributions of property instead of cash) during the fund's life. We'll discuss distributions in kind in more detail in Chapter 7. As you can imagine, distributions in kind are more common in venture funds and less common in real estate funds. LPs do not typically want distributions of apartment complexes.

17. GP CLAWBACK

Clawbacks require the GP to return any excess carried interest to the fund. Clawbacks are common in closed-end funds. We'll discuss clawbacks in detail in Chapter 7.

18. LIMITED PARTNER ADVISORY COMMITTEE (LPAC)

Many funds have a Limited Partner Advisory Committee (LPAC) made up of the largest (or most strategic) LPs. The LPAC can approve certain actions under the fund documents and provide guidance to the GP. However, except as mentioned below, LPACs typically do not make investment-related decisions. The fund's investment committee and LPAC are usually separate.

Matters requiring LPAC approval might include:

- Making an investment that would otherwise be prohibited
- Approving a transaction between the GP and the fund
- Extending the fund term or the investment period
- Ending a suspension period

An LPAC can be very helpful for the GP. In most cases, the LPs as a whole (voting based on commitments) can approve any of the matters above. However, taking a full LP vote is burdensome. By creating an LPAC of three to five engaged (and friendly) LPs, the GP can get things approved much faster and more easily.

19. REPORTS TO LPS

What financial and other informational reports will be given to LPs? What are the time limits for producing and distributing them? Many funds provide annual financials, quarterly financials, and K-1s. They also provide general updates and market reports.

While some funds are required to provide audited annual financial statements, many funds are not required by law to have their financials audited. However, at a certain fund size (around $30–50 million), LPs will start demanding an audit.

Take a look at Chapters 14 and 15 to determine whether your fund or syndication is required by law to have audited financials. In general, real estate and venture capital funds are less likely to need an audit than private equity, private credit, and hedge funds.

20. AMENDMENTS

How will amendments be handled? Most funds require a majority of the LPs (based on commitments) to approve LPA amendments. Often, the GP can make simple administrative updates without LP approval. Typically, the LPAC doesn't have the power to approve amendments.

In practice, most proposed amendments are handled via a formal LP consent process where your lawyer prepares a document to send to your LPs and tallies the results. In some cases, the LPA might deem a failure by an LP to respond within a certain time period (such as fifteen days) to be an automatic approval of the proposed amendment.

Now you know all the essential terms...except one. Next up, let's tackle the trickiest term of all: the distribution waterfall.

CHAPTER 7

How Do You Distribute Money to Investors Using a "Waterfall"?

We can't put this off any longer. It's time to discuss the cornerstone of fund economics: the carried interest. As discussed in Chapter 2, the carried interest (also sometimes called "promote" or "incentive income") is the GP's share of the profits earned by the fund. Carried interest is *not* guaranteed. The GP earns carried interest only if the fund is profitable.

HOW IS CARRIED INTEREST TAXED?

Carried interest is typically taxed at capital gains rates, so long as certain requirements are met. We'll discuss this more in Chapter 16. The tax treatment of carried interest is a frequent topic of heated debate by politicians, with some arguing that carried interest should be taxed at ordinary income rates (like management fees).

HOW DOES THE GP GET CARRIED INTEREST?

Every investment fund or syndication has a Distributions section in its governing documents. It's usually somewhere in the middle. The Distributions section is often called the "distribution waterfall." If the fund has money to distribute, the distribution waterfall dictates how the cash is divided among the fund's LPs and the GP. In this chapter, we'll walk through five examples of different types of distribution waterfalls.

WATERFALL WALKTHROUGH #1: SIMPLE SYNDICATION

This first walkthrough is for a simple syndication.

Simple Waterfall
(One Investment)

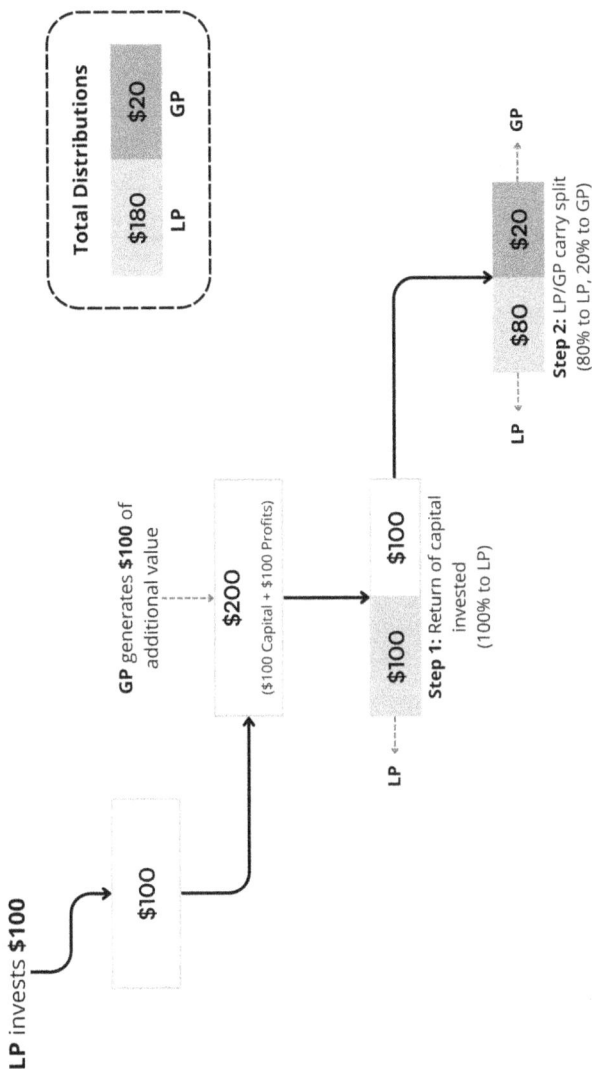

LP invests $100

$100

GP generates **$100** of additional value

$200
($100 Capital + $100 Profits)

Step 1: Return of capital invested
(100% to LP)

LP ⤍ $100 | $100

Step 2: LP/GP carry split
(80% to LP, 20% to GP)

LP ⤍ $80 | $20 ⤏ GP

Total Distributions

$180
LP

$20
GP

Let's assume the LPs invested $100. The syndication successfully sold the investment for 2x and now has $200 to distribute among the investors. The above waterfall would be common for a single-asset syndication in venture capital. This vehicle may have been formed to purchase Series A stock in a tech company.

How Would This Waterfall Be Written in a Legal Document?

This waterfall might appear in the fund's governing documents as follows:

If there is any money to distribute, it shall be distributed as follows:

- *Step 1: 100 percent to the LP until they have received distributions equal to their capital contributions; and*
- *Step 2: 80 percent to the LP, and 20 percent to the GP.*

Note: This simplified example assumes the GP did not invest any money alongside the LPs.

How Would Money Be Distributed Among the GP and LP Pursuant to This Waterfall?

Now, let's examine each step of the waterfall in this example:

- **Capital Contribution:** The initial $100 capital contribution by the LP.
- **Sale:** The syndication sells the assets for $200.
- **Waterfall Step #1:** Per the first step in the waterfall, the LP must be reimbursed the full amount of their capital contribution before any other distributions can be made—in this case, $100.
- **Waterfall Step #2:** After returning that $100, there's still $100 left to be distributed ($200 − $100 = $100). Pursuant to the second step in the waterfall, profits (after the return of capi-

tal) are to be split 80 percent to the LP and 20 percent to the GP. So, we send $80 to the LP and $20 to the GP.

The $20 received by the GP is their carried interest.

CAN YOU DISTRIBUTE ASSETS OTHER THAN CASH?

Most fund agreements have a provision called "distributions in kind" that allows funds to distribute property other than cash. This is most common in funds purchasing securities and less common in funds buying illiquid assets. A multifamily real estate fund typically wouldn't distribute apartment buildings to its investors. A private equity fund wouldn't distribute an HVAC company.

LIMITS ON DISTRIBUTIONS IN KIND

Even in securities funds, there are typically restrictions on distributions in kind. For example, many funds limit distributions in kind during the fund's life to freely tradeable securities (e.g., unrestricted public stock). Only after the fund's term has ended can restricted private stock be distributed.

EXAMPLE—SERIES C PREFERRED

If a fund has Series C Preferred stock, it would typically not be able to distribute that stock in kind to investors until the end of the fund's life...unless the underlying company goes public. If the company goes public, the fund's Series C Preferred stock would be converted into standard common stock trading on the NYSE or NASDAQ. At that point, the fund could distribute the common stock to investors immediately. It wouldn't need to wait until the end of the fund's life.

In fact, LPs often prefer that funds distribute the publicly traded stock instead of holding it within the fund. Sometimes, VCs (venture capital funds) hold on to public shares because they want to (potentially) earn carried interest on the post-initial public offering appreciation. LPs don't like that (big surprise).

AMERICAN VS. EUROPEAN WATERFALLS

Waterfall Walkthrough #1: Simple Syndication, above, explained how a single-asset syndication might distribute its profits. But how do you distribute profits if you have a multi-asset investment fund? There are two main types of distribution waterfalls used by funds with more than one asset:

- European waterfall (also known as "netted" or "crossed")
- American waterfall (also known as "deal-by-deal")

While I assume that, at some point, American waterfalls were common in America and European waterfalls were common in Europe, that is no longer the case. Paradoxically, most funds in the United States have a European waterfall.

EUROPEAN WATERFALLS

European waterfalls are simple enough. All the capital contributions made by an LP are treated as one big, fungible pool of money that must be returned to the LP before the GP gets any carried interest. In other words, the capital contributions among all investments are "netted" or "crossed."

Waterfall Walkthrough #2: European Waterfall

This example assumes a very simple waterfall, which is common in venture capital funds.

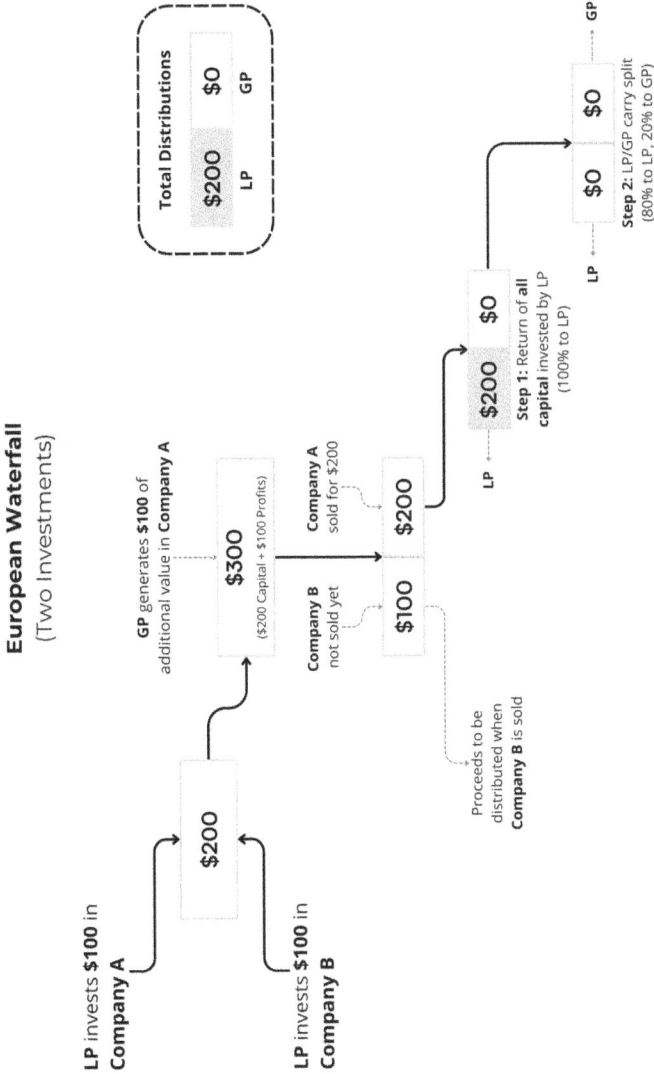

European Waterfall
(Two Investments)

LP invests **$100** in **Company A**

LP invests **$100** in **Company B**

$200

GP generates **$100** of additional value in **Company A**

$300
($200 Capital + $100 Profits)

Company A sold for $200

Company B not sold yet

$200

$100

Proceeds to be distributed when **Company B** is sold

LP ⇢ $200 $0

Step 1: Return of all **capital** invested by LP (100% to LP)

LP ⇢ $0 $0 ⇢ GP

Step 2: LP/GP carry split (80% to LP, 20% to GP)

Total Distributions

$200 $0
LP   GP

· 87 ·

How Would This Waterfall Be Written in a Legal Document?

This waterfall might appear in the fund's governing documents as follows:

If there is any money to distribute, it shall be distributed as follows:

- **Step 1:** *100 percent to the LP until the LP gets a return of their capital contributions used to fund all investments; and*
- **Step 2:** *80 percent to the LP, and 20 percent to the GP.*

How Would Money Be Distributed Among the GP and LP Pursuant to This Waterfall?

Let's walk through how the money flows in this example:

- **Capital Contribution:** The initial capital contributions by the LP of $200 ($100 was used to buy Company A, and $100 was used to buy Company B).
- **Sale:** The fund sells Company A for $200.
- **Waterfall Step #1:** Per the first step in the waterfall, $200 (the total capital invested by the LP) goes to the LP.
- **Waterfall Step #2:** We don't have any more money to distribute, so we don't get to the second step in the waterfall, and the GP does not get any carried interest yet. No fun!

Note that if the fund had sold Company A for more than $200, the GP would have received some carried interest. For example, if the fund had sold Company A for $225, $200 would have been returned to the LP, and the remaining $25 would have been split 80 percent to the LP ($20) and 20 percent to the GP ($5).

Assuming Company B is successfully sold for more than $0, the GP will receive carried interest from its sale (because the LP already received a total return of capital upon the sale of Company A).

Returning Capital Contributions for Fund Expenses in European Waterfalls

Returning expenses is simple in European waterfalls. In Waterfall Walkthrough #2: European Waterfall, we oversimplified Step 1, saying the LP gets back all its capital contributions used to fund all investments.

In reality, LPs get back all their capital contributions used to fund...anything. It looks something more like:

- *Step 1: 100 percent to the LP until the LP gets back all their capital contributions used for any purpose; and*
- *Step 2: 80 percent to the LP, and 20 percent to the GP.*

In other words, if an LP invests $100, $90 of which is used to fund investments, $8 of which is used to pay the management fee, and $2 of which is used to pay other fund expenses, the LP would receive the full $100 in Step 1 of the European waterfall.

AMERICAN WATERFALLS

American waterfalls are a bit trickier, but I'm confident you'll get it! Unlike European waterfalls, American waterfalls calculate returns on a deal-by-deal basis. In other words, an LP's capital contributions used to fund different deals are segregated in the waterfall.

Waterfall Walkthrough #3: American Waterfall

This example assumes a simple American waterfall.

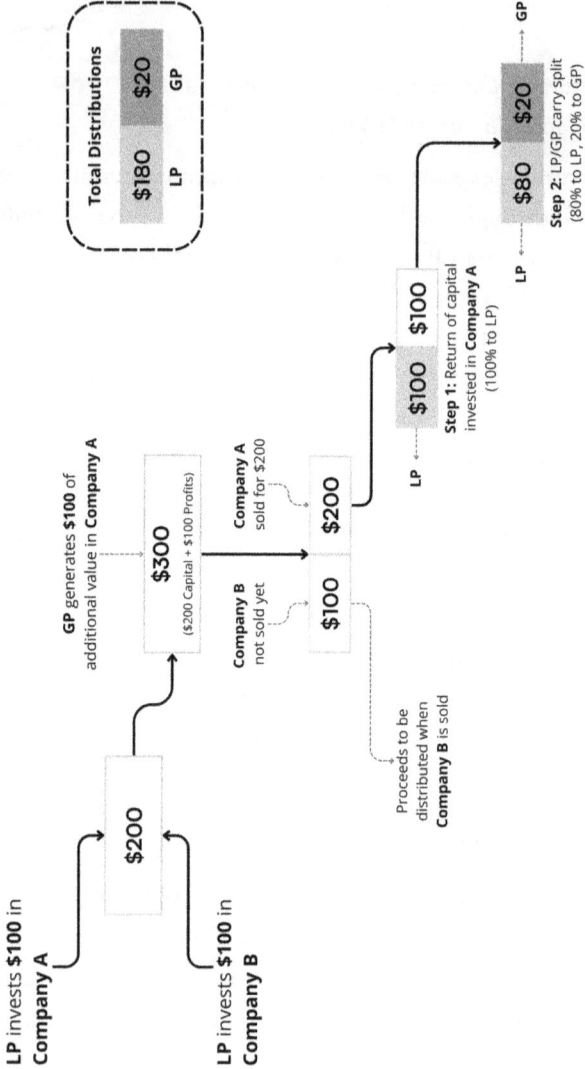

American Waterfall
(Two Investments)

LP invests **$100** in **Company A**

LP invests **$100** in **Company B**

$200

GP generates **$100** of additional value in **Company A**

$300
($200 Capital + $100 Profits)

Company A sold for $200

Company B not sold yet

$200 $100

Proceeds to be distributed when **Company B** is sold

LP $100 $100

Step 1: Return of capital invested in **Company A** (100% to LP)

LP $80 $20   GP

Step 2: LP/GP carry split (80% to LP, 20% to GP)

Total Distributions

$180 $20
LP   GP

How Would This Waterfall Be Written in a Legal Document?

This waterfall might appear in the fund's governing documents as follows:

If there is any money to distribute from the sale of an investment, it shall be distributed as follows:

- *Step 1: 100 percent to the LP until the LP gets a return of their capital contributions used to fund the sold investment; and*
- *Step 2: 80 percent to the LP, and 20 percent to the GP.*

Note that Step 1 is different than in a European waterfall! It refers to a return of capital used for the investment that was sold—not a return of capital from all investments.

How Would Money Be Distributed Among the GP and LP Pursuant to This Waterfall?

Let's walk through how the money flows in this example (the first two bullets are the same as Waterfall Walkthrough #2: European Waterfall):

- **Capital Contribution:** The initial capital contributions by the LP of $200 ($100 was used to buy Company A, and $100 was used to buy Company B).
- **Sale:** The fund sells Company A for $200.
- **Waterfall Step #1:** Per the first step in the waterfall, $100 (the total capital invested by the LP to fund the purchase of Company A) goes to the LP.
- **Waterfall Step #2:** The remaining $100 is split 80 percent to the LP ($80) and 20 percent to the GP ($20).

As you can see, the American waterfall is better for the GP. With the exact same facts, the American waterfall yields $20 of carried interest, while the European waterfall results in a big ol' goose egg.

Returning Capital Contributions for Fund Expenses in American Waterfalls

There are a couple of options for returning expenses in American waterfalls.

Option 1: Return All Expenses

The more LP-friendly formulation is to return all fund expenses in Step 1 of the waterfall. It might look like this:

- *Step 1: 100 percent to the LP until the LP gets a return of their capital contributions used to fund the sold investment plus all capital contributions used to fund expenses; and*
- *Step 2: 80 percent to the LP, and 20 percent to the GP.*

Option 2: Return Investment-Related Expenses

The more GP-friendly option allocates fund expenses on an investment-by-investment basis and only returns expenses allocated to the sold investment. It might look like this:

- *Step 1: 100 percent to the LP until the LP gets a return of their capital contributions used to fund the sold investment plus all capital contributions used to fund expenses allocable to the sold investment; and*
- *Step 2: 80 percent to the LP, and 20 percent to the GP.*

"Deal-by-Deal" vs. "Realized Investments" in American Waterfalls

A final wrinkle is that some American waterfalls aren't really "deal-by-deal" after all. Instead of strictly segregating deals, the first step of these waterfalls returns all capital contributed to all fund investments that have been sold or permanently written off.

Let's say you have five investments. You sold Investment #1 yesterday. When you sold that investment, Step 1 of the waterfall required a return of LP capital used to fund Investment #1. This is what we did in Waterfall Walkthrough #3: American Waterfall.

Today, you sell Investment #2. Now, Step 1 of the waterfall requires you to return capital used to fund Investment #1 *and* Investment #2—both investments have been disposed of. But you do not consider capital contributions to fund Investments #3–5 because they haven't been sold or written off yet. You'll deal with them later.

It's kind of a hybrid between a netted waterfall and a true deal-by-deal waterfall. It's basically a European waterfall but only for exited investments.

It might look something like this:

- *Step 1: 100 percent to the LP until the LP gets a return of their capital contributions used to fund all investments that have been sold or completely written off plus all capital contributions used to fund expenses; and*
- *Step 2: 80 percent to the LP, and 20 percent to the GP.*

As you can see, there are many options for American waterfalls!

SELECTING A WATERFALL—AMERICAN OR EUROPEAN?

While American waterfalls are better for GPs, European waterfalls are more common in the market. For that reason, I often advise emerging managers to go with a European waterfall. In addition, American waterfalls are more likely to result in an unfavorable clawback situation (we'll discuss clawbacks later in this chapter). Using American waterfalls is not unreasonable, but having a European waterfall is more LP-friendly and will likely make fundraising easier.

PREFERRED RETURNS

Now that we've discussed European versus American waterfalls, we're going to move on to a separate topic in investment fund waterfalls. In many funds (especially real estate and private equity funds), the waterfall has more steps than the simple two-step waterfalls we've discussed so far in this chapter.

After (or sometimes before) the "return of capital" step, LPs might receive a preferred return before the GP gets their carried interest. This could be the case in a syndication, a fund with a European waterfall, or a fund with an American waterfall. In the walkthrough below, the preferred return will be applied to a simple syndication (to make things as simple as possible).

WATERFALL WALKTHROUGH #4: PREFERRED RETURN

In this example, the LP receives an 8 percent preferred return before the GP starts earning carried interest.

Waterfall with Preferred Return
(No GP Catch-Up)

LP invests **$100**

$100

GP generates **$100** of additional value

$200
($100 Capital + $100 Profits)

LP

$100 $100

Step 1: Return of capital invested
(100% to LP)

LP

$8 $92

Step 2: LP receives preferred return
(8% to LP)

LP

$73.60 $18.40

Step 3: LP/GP carry split
(80% to LP, 20% to GP)

GP

Total Distributions

$181.60 $18.40
LP GP

Assumptions:
- 8% preferred return
- Investment sold after 1 year

How Would This Waterfall Be Written in a Legal Document?

This waterfall might appear in the fund's governing documents as follows:

If there is any money to distribute, it shall be distributed as follows:

- **Step 1:** *100 percent to the LP until they have received distributions equal to their capital contributions;*
- **Step 2:** *100 percent to the LP until they have received distributions equal to 8 percent, compounded annually, on their capital contributions; and*
- **Step 3:** *80 percent to the LP, and 20 percent to the GP.*

In short, if the fund returns capital to the LP but does not exceed their contributions plus an 8 percent return, the GP does not get any carried interest.

How Would Money Be Distributed Among the GP and LP Pursuant to This Waterfall?

Let's walk through the flow of funds in this example:

- **Capital Contribution:** The initial capital contributions by the LP of $100.
- **Sale:** The fund sells the assets for $200.
- **Waterfall Step #1:** Per the first step in the waterfall, $100 (the full amount of LP's capital contributions) goes to the LP.
- **Waterfall Step #2:** Per the second step in the waterfall, the LP gets an 8 percent return on its $100 contribution. Here, let's assume it's been one year since the LP contributed the capital, so the preferred return is $8 (8 percent of $100).
- **Waterfall Step #3:** The remaining $92 is split 80 percent to the LP ($73.60) and 20 percent to the GP ($18.40).

In total, the LP received $181.60 (100 + 8 + 73.6), and the

GP received $18.40. If there were no preferred return, the LP would have received $180 (a capital return of $100 plus 80 percent of the remaining $100), and the GP would have received $20. So, obviously, the preferred return is good for the LP.

DIFFERENT FLAVORS OF PREFERRED RETURNS

Here are a few ways preferred returns can differ from fund to fund:

- **Compounded/Non-Compounded:** In some funds, the preferred return compounds annually. In other funds, it is a "simple" (non-compounded) preferred return.
- **Percentage:** In lower-risk funds, the preferred return is often lower. For example, in a buy-and-hold multifamily real estate fund, the preferred return might be just 6 percent. In higher-risk funds, the preferred return is usually higher. For example, a development fund might have a preferred return of 12 percent.
- **Positioning Within the Waterfall:** Some funds have the preferred return step after the return of capital step. Others have the preferred return step before the return of capital step.
- **Dual Waterfalls:** Some funds have a standard waterfall, as we discussed above for dispositions (sales, refinances, etc.), but a separate waterfall for cash flow from operations. The cash flow waterfall might have no return of capital step at all. Step 1 would be the preferred return, and Step 2 would be a profit split. This is more common in buy-and-hold style funds.

GP CATCH-UPS

On to the next topic! Many funds and syndications with a preferred return also have something called a "GP catch-up" after the preferred return step in the waterfall. People always get confused by this one. Let's start with some philosophy and then look at an example.

WHY DO YOU NEED GP CATCH-UPS?

In a distribution waterfall, the profit split is the percentage of the profits the GP is supposed to get as carried interest. Simple enough. But if you look at Waterfall Walkthrough #4: Preferred Return, the GP didn't get 20 percent of the profits at all! The GP got 18.4 percent, even though the ultimate "profit split" was 20 percent. This is because the LP got a priority distribution (the preferred return) before the profit split kicked in.

A GP catchup is a provision that "catches the GP up" to the 80/20 profit split after the preferred return but before the official 80/20 step of the waterfall. An 80/20 waterfall can be thought of like this: "For every four steps forward the LP takes, the GP takes one step forward." The preferred return is the LP taking their four steps forward early. The GP catchup is the GP taking one step forward before the final phase of the LP and GP taking their steps forward simultaneously. Otherwise, the GP will always be one step behind.

WATERFALL WALKTHROUGH #5: GP CATCHUP

Here's the same waterfall as the previous one in Waterfall Walkthrough #4: Preferred Return, but with a GP catchup added.

Waterfall with Preferred Return
(With GP Catch-Up)

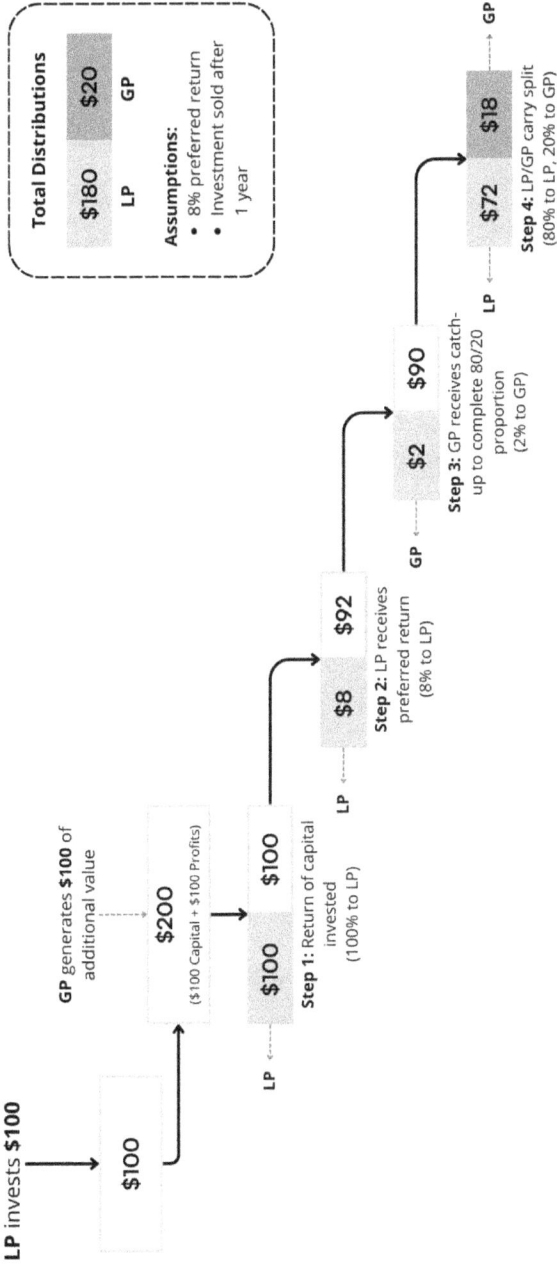

LP invests **$100**

$100

GP generates **$100** of additional value

$200
($100 Capital + $100 Profits)

$100	$100

Step 1: Return of capital invested
(100% to LP)
LP

$8	$92

Step 2: LP receives preferred return
(8% to LP)
LP

$2	$90

Step 3: GP receives catch-up to complete 80/20 proportion
(2% to GP)
GP

$72	$18

Step 4: LP/GP carry split
(80% to LP, 20% to GP)
LP   GP

Total Distributions

$180	$20
LP	GP

Assumptions:
- 8% preferred return
- Investment sold after 1 year

· 99 ·

This waterfall might appear in the fund's governing documents as follows:

If there is any money to distribute, it shall be distributed as follows:

- *Step 1:* 100 *percent to the LP until they have received distributions equal to their capital contributions;*
- *Step 2:* 100 *percent to the LP until they have received distributions equal to 8 percent, compounded annually, on their capital contributions;*
- *Step 3:* 100 *percent to the GP until the GP has received 20 percent of the amounts distributed pursuant to Step 2 and Step 3; and*
- *Step 4:* 80 *percent to the LP, and 20 percent to the GP.*

How Would Money Be Distributed Among the GP and LP Pursuant to This Waterfall?

Let's walk through the flow of funds in this example:

- **Capital Contribution:** The initial capital contributions by the LP of $100.
- **Sale:** The fund sells the assets for $200.
- **Waterfall Step #1:** Per the first step in the waterfall, $100 (the full amount of LP's capital contributions) goes to the LP.
- **Waterfall Step #2:** Per the second step in the waterfall, the LP gets an 8 percent return on its $100 contribution. Here, let's assume it's been one year since the LP contributed the capital, so the preferred return is $8 (8 percent of $100).
- **Waterfall Step #3:** The GP catchup kicks in. Because the profit split in Step #4 allocates 20 percent of the profits

to the GP, this step catches the GP up to 20 percent of the profits distributed so far (in Step #2 and this Step #3). Here, the GP gets $2 because $2 is 20 percent of $10—the sum of $8 (the profits distributed to the LP in Step 2) and $2 (the profits distributed to the GP in this step).

- **Waterfall Step #4:** Per the fourth step in the waterfall, the remaining $90 ($100 – 8 – 2) is split 80 percent to the LP ($72) and 20 percent to the GP ($18).

In total, the LP received $180 (100 + 8 + 72), and the GP received $20 (2 + 18). The GP catchup resulted in the GP getting more carried interest than they would have without the GP catchup. In fact, the GP got the same amount of carried interest as if there were no preferred return at all (as long as the fund returns at least 10 percent).

This setup results in the following:

- **Poor Performance:** If the fund generates less than a 10 percent return (8 percent for the preferred return and 2 percent for the GP catchup), the GP makes less money than if there were no preferred return and GP catchup.
- **Good Performance:** If the fund generates at least 10 percent, the GP makes the same amount of money as if there were no preferred return and GP catchup, but the LP gets the money first in time, which benefits LPs.

DIFFERENT FLAVORS OF GP CATCHUPS

Our above example has a 100 percent GP catchup, which means the GP gets 100 percent of the distributions in Step 3 until the GP has received 20 percent of the profits. Another option (which is more favorable to LPs) is to have a catchup of less than 100 percent.

For example, Step 3 could give 50 percent of the profits to the LP and 50 percent to the GP until the GP has received 20 percent of the profits. This is still better than no catchup at all from the GP's perspective, but it's less exciting than the 100 percent catchup. It just takes longer for the GP to catch up.

⚠ FUND TRAP #7: NOT TAKING THE WATERFALL SERIOUSLY

You'd be surprised, but some GPs don't take sufficient care when crafting their waterfalls. Carried interest is the big reason people start a fund or syndication. GPs should carefully evaluate different waterfall options in the context of their asset class and return profile.

The waterfall also has ramifications for a GP's public image. Do you really want to be the GP charging 50 percent carried interest? You might make excess profits in the short term, but, unless you're Renaissance Technologies, it probably isn't a great long-term strategy.

One time, a potential client wanted us to read their fund documents to make sure they were ok. Alas, they were not ok. The Distributions section of the LPA said: "Distributions will be made pro rata to the partners." In other words, the provision granting the GP carried interest was…gone.

Absent! Forgotten! Missing!

The LPA is the legal document governing the relationship between the GP and the LPs, so if the carried interest isn't mentioned in the LPA, there's a good argument to be made that the GP isn't entitled to it (even if carried interest was mentioned in the marketing deck or PPM). I'll leave it to the litigators to decide how this particular case would shake out, but my warning is clear.

CLAWBACKS

Don't break out the lobster until you're sure you won't have a clawback. A clawback is a provision that requires the fund to "re-test" the waterfall at the end of the fund's life. You consider all the capital contributions and all the distributions to determine whether the GP got too much carried interest.

If the GP did get too much carried interest, they must return the excess to the fund (this is the "clawing back" of the carry). How does a GP get too much carried interest?

Let's say we have a very simple European waterfall with an 80/20 split after a return of LP capital and an LP commitment of $100. The GP calls $50 (50 percent of the LP's commitment). The investment ends up being a success (a 2x multiple), and the fund distributes $100. The first step in the waterfall is the return of $50 (the LP's invested capital). The second step of the waterfall is an 80/20 split of the profits, so $40 goes to the LP and $10 goes to the GP as carried interest.

Next, the GP calls the remaining $50 (the second half of the LP's commitment) and invests it. The investment completely implodes and is a total loss. Nothing to distribute. Sad day.

The clawback re-tests the waterfall at the end of the fund's life and sees $100 of total capital contributions and $100 of total distributions. What "should" have happened per the waterfall is the LP receives $100 as a return of capital and the GP gets nothing.

But wait!

The GP took $10 of carried interest after selling the first investment (before evaporating the second $50 investment). The clawback says the GP has to put the $10 back into the fund, which is then distributed to LPs.

Clawbacks can be an especially big deal for funds with American waterfalls because American waterfalls result in GPs taking carried interest earlier in the fund's life than European waterfalls (see Waterfall Walkthroughs #2 and #3, above). So, the GP could take lots of carried interest from the good deals early on (hooray) but then have lackluster deals thereafter (boo). When the waterfall is re-tested at the end of the fund's life, there could be a serious clawback waiting, and the GP may need to return carried interest. In fact, because of the clawback, at the end of a fund's life, the American waterfall is no longer better for GPs than the European waterfall.

DIFFERENT FLAVORS OF CLAWBACK

In some cases, LPs might negotiate for the following:

- **Personal Guarantees:** Technically, the GP entity (typically an LLC) is what's on the hook for the clawback. Sophisticated LPs may insist the individual fund principals guarantee the clawback obligation.
- **Multiple Clawbacks:** This isn't super common, but some hard-negotiating LPs will require multiple clawback "tests" throughout the fund's life. For example, a clawback after year seven and again at the end of the fund's life.
- **Carry Escrow:** In some cases, the GP may be required to put a percentage of their carried interest in an escrow account so it's easier to claw back. The GP finally gets the carried interest once it's clear there won't be a clawback situation.

Now that you've mastered distribution waterfalls, it's time to learn where all these fund terms go. In the next chapter, we'll discuss the legal document you need to successfully raise a fund or syndication.

CHAPTER 8

What Legal Documents Do You Need to Raise a Fund?

Once you've decided on the structure and terms of your fund or syndication, you need to formalize your offering. In this chapter, we'll discuss the key legal documents you need to raise an investment fund or syndication. We'll divide the documents into two main categories:

- **Principal Fund Documents:** These are the main, large documents investors will review.
- **Ancillary Fund Documents:** These are internal documents, which are more boilerplate and less exciting.

PRINCIPAL FUND DOCUMENTS

First, let's hit the big-ticket items. These are the substantive documents LPs will review (and in some cases sign) before investing.

1. SUMMARY OF TERMS

Your summary of terms lists the high-level terms you chose in Chapter 6. Don't be fooled though, it's often quite detailed. A summary of terms might be five to ten pages for a simple syndication and ten to twenty pages for a multi-asset investment fund. If you have a PPM (discussed below), your summary of terms will be in the PPM. If you don't have a PPM, you'll typically give your summary of terms to prospective LPs as a standalone document in your data room.

As discussed in Chapter 1, you might choose to circulate your summary of terms, along with your marketing deck, as your primary marketing materials before working with your lawyer to draft the remaining long-form legal documents discussed in this chapter.

Typically, nobody signs the summary of terms. It's just an informational document.

2. LIMITED PARTNERSHIP AGREEMENT (LPA)

The LPA is the main legal contract between the GP and the LPs. In a simple syndication, it might be thirty-five to forty pages long. A multi-asset fund might have an LPA of eighty to one hundred pages or more. The LPA is essentially the expanded, fancy, legalese version of your summary of terms.

In most cases, the LPA signed at your fund's initial closing date will be the "Amended and Restated LPA." Early in the fund-formation process, your lawyer will typically draft a very short "initial LPA" that will enable you to formally set up the fund entity (usually a limited partnership), open bank accounts, and otherwise prepare for the initial closing. At the initial closing, everyone will enter into the long-form Amended and Restated LPA.

Throughout this book, I refer to this document as the LPA. However, if your fund or syndication is an LLC (instead of a limited partnership), this agreement is technically called the LLC Agreement or the Operating Agreement (as LLCs don't have LPAs). These are all synonyms for the same thing: the contract between the GP and the LPs.

In many funds, the GP signs the LPA both on their own behalf and on behalf of the LPs via a power of attorney granted in the subscription documents (discussed below). In other funds, all LPs sign the LPA (though this is uncommon in institutional-grade funds and syndications).

⚠ FUND TRAP #8: CUTTING CORNERS ON LEGAL DOCUMENTS

This is an admittedly self-serving statement, but you absolutely must work with experts to draft your fund or syndication documents. If you fail to do so, you might accidentally run afoul of laws and regulations. In addition, your legal documents may not reflect the deal you thought you were making with LPs. This happens more than you might think.

People often come to the firm where I work to have us "fix" their fund. In one instance, a fund manager (who had miraculously already raised two funds) had used a "general practitioner" to set up their first two investment funds, and they came to regret it. They thought they were going to fund part of their GP commitment with an acquisition fee waiver (see Chapter 16), but the required language was nowhere to be found in the legal documents. Also, the carried interest waterfall was switched, with the LPs getting 30 percent of the profits and the GP getting 70 percent. These mistakes can (usually) be fixed, but it involves amending the LPA with your tail between your legs (and admitting to LPs that you—or your lawyer—were careless).

The fund documents are the deal between the GP and the LPs. If you screw those up, the whole fund might be in jeopardy. Take this seriously!

3. SUBSCRIPTION DOCUMENTS (SUB DOCS)

The subscription documents are what LPs sign to officially invest in your fund or syndication. The sub docs usually have a few key sections:

- **Representations and Warranties:** The LPs agree to a long list of representations and warranties for the benefit of the GP and their affiliates.
- **Investor Questionnaire:** LPs answer questions about their backgrounds, wealth, and the vehicles through which they're investing (if they're not investing in their individual capacity). The questionnaire is necessary so the fund can comply with the laws and regulations we'll discuss in Part II.
- **Signature Pages:** LPs indicate their investment amounts. In many funds, they also sign a power of attorney entitling the GP to sign the LPA on their behalf.
- **Disclosure Statement:** If the fund does not have a PPM, the subscription documents should contain all the required legal disclosures and risk factors. See the section on PPMs below.

4. PRIVATE PLACEMENT MEMORANDUM (PPM)

The PPM is a big, fancy marketing document. It looks very official. It is, however, not strictly necessary.

The PPM has a split personality. The first half of the document is filled with flowery language, positive vibes, and delightful graphs describing how great the GP is. But then...there's a sudden shift. The second half of the PPM is depressed, nervous, and timid. You learn that investing is risky, and there are 101 ways to lose your money.

Raising Money Without a PPM

Some smaller funds and syndications raise money without a PPM. The scary legal stuff is necessary, though. If you forego a PPM, you should put the legal disclosures and risk factors in the subscription agreement so investors can review them before deciding to invest. The positive marketing language can go into your marketing deck. As such, the deck becomes your sword, and the disclosures in the sub docs your shield.

In practice, many funds still choose to have a full PPM (especially larger funds and those relying on the 506(c) exemption under the Securities Act—discussed in Chapter 12).

Complex Fund Structures

If you have special regulatory or tax requirements that result in you needing to form a parallel fund, feeder fund, or other alternative investment vehicle, you will generally need a separate LPA and sub docs for each vehicle. In many cases, the PPMs can be combined. You'll also need to set up separate legal entities (and potentially draft ancillary documents) for each parallel or feeder vehicle.

ANCILLARY FUND DOCUMENTS

In addition to the delightful documents discussed above, you'll likely need some or all of the following side documents:

- **Marketing Deck:** A slide deck (or similar) that outlines your thesis, track record, and fund terms. You should have your lawyer review this before sending it to prospective investors. See Chapter 1 for more information.

- **Management Agreement:** If you have both a GP and a ManCo, you'll often have a short agreement that designates the ManCo as the fund's management company in exchange for receiving the management fee. If the GP and ManCo are unaffiliated (less common), this agreement can be quite long and negotiated.

- **Entity Formation Documents:** You must form the fund entities. The documents to do so generally include state formation certificates, foreign qualifications, employer identification numbers, and initial governing agreements.

- **Comprehensive GP/ManCo Documents:** If you aren't a sole GP, you likely want robust documents laying out the deal between you and the other fund principals (including anyone who will receive carried interest). These documents describe what happens if someone dies, gets divorced, leaves the firm, or commits a bad act.

- **Rule 506 "Covered Person" Questionnaire:** If you're using Regulation D, you may want a document signed by the fund's principals confirming they aren't disqualified from using Regulation D due to a financial crime, SEC action, or FINRA ban.

- **Closing Resolutions:** This is a blanket "consent" document that authorizes and ratifies everything the GP did to set up the fund and admit investors.

Obviously, this isn't a comprehensive list—for that, work with your lawyer! We'll talk through the mechanics of holding your initial closing and admitting LPs in Chapter 10.

At this point, you've collaborated with your lawyer to create impeccable documents you're ready to send out to potential investors. But what if the investors want to negotiate the terms of the fund documents? We'll cover negotiation strategies in the next chapter.

CHAPTER 9

How Do You Negotiate with Potential Investors?

In this chapter, we'll discuss everyone's favorite topic: negotiation tactics. After the GP finishes the first draft of the fund documents, they send the documents to potential LPs and cross their fingers. At this point, the LPs have three options:

1. Invest
2. Don't invest
3. Indicate interest, but negotiate for better terms

TO DEAL OR NOT TO DEAL?

If an LP chooses Door #3 above and attempts to negotiate, the GP has three options:

1. Decline the attempt to negotiate ("Take it or leave it!")
2. Change the terms of the LPA
3. Enter into a "side letter" with one or more LP

CHANGING THE TERMS OF THE FUND DOCUMENTS

The simplest way to negotiate is to revise the fund documents.

For example, let's say the fund has a management fee percentage of 2 percent, but an LP wants a management fee percentage of 1.5 percent. The GP could revise the LPA, changing the definition of "management fee percentage" from 2 percent to 1.5 percent. Easy!

In this example, the new 1.5 percent management fee percentage would apply to all LPs in the fund. It's a major change to the GP's fee income (a fund-wide haircut on fees).

SIDE LETTERS

Changing the fund documents to appease one LP as described above is like using a flamethrower to kill a housefly. It's not targeted and may result in collateral damage. If you have one LP who wants a fee reduction from 2 percent to 1.5 percent, why not give just that single LP a fee reduction?

You can! You just need a side letter. A side letter is a bilateral contract between the fund and a single LP where the LP gets special rights not granted to the other LPs.

HOW TO NEGOTIATE SIDE LETTERS

Let's take a deep dive into the exclusive, bespoke club of side-letter negotiations.

WHEN ARE SIDE LETTERS NEGOTIATED?

In many cases, LPs present their side-letter requests to the fund early in the negotiation process. Sophisticated LPs often have a "form" side letter they send to every fund. If you're an LP in a lot of deals, you might consider working with your lawyer to draft a form side letter.

After the LP sends their form side letter, the GP and LP typically negotiate the LPA and the side letter in parallel. In certain cases, some side-letter requests might make their way into the LPA itself and vice versa, as discussed below.

GP STRATEGIES FOR SIDE-LETTER ADMINISTRATION

If you aren't careful, side letters can get out of control. Three ways to reduce your side-letter nightmares include:

- **Decline Side Letters:** Don't be afraid to "just say no" if an LP asks for a side letter. In many cases (especially where the fund/syndication is in high demand), the investor will capitulate. This is also true if the investor is a small percentage of the total investor base. An LP investing $100,000 in a $50 million fund should not get a side letter.
- **Avoid MFNs:** Don't give out most-favored nations provisions (MFNs) like Halloween candy (I wrote this sentence in October, and it made sense then). You should aim to give out zero to one MFNs per fund or syndication. We'll discuss MFNs in about two minutes.
- **Copy + Paste:** If multiple LPs ask for the same provision (for example, an "affiliate transfer" provision), give everyone the exact same language. Once you have a provision you're happy with, use it as the model for all your side letters. The LPs will understand. We do this in every fund we raise for GPs.

WHAT DO INVESTORS PUT IN SIDE LETTERS?

LP side-letter requests typically fall into two overall buckets:

- **Preferential Terms:** These are provisions like fee discounts or special information rights that put the LP in a preferred position. They may or may not be in the LP's form side-letter request.
- **Investor-Specific Administrative Terms:** These provisions are in the LP's form side-letter request, and they aren't very exciting. They're necessary for the LP to comply with applicable laws, regulations, or tax requirements.

Let's look at some examples of each.

Sample Preferential Terms in Side Letters
1. Most-Favored Nations (MFN)

This is arguably the most powerful side-letter provision possible. If an LP has an MFN provision, they have the right to peek at all the other LPs' side letters and take provisions for their own side letter. It's a side-letter buffet! So, if another LP has a carried interest reduction from 20 percent to 15 percent, the LP with an MFN can swipe that carry reduction for themselves! Now, both LPs have a carry percentage of 15 percent.

In practice, MFNs are often subject to restrictions, such as the following:

- **Investment Size:** The MFN does not entitle the LP to look at side letters between the fund and LPs investing more than the LP with the MFN.
- **Affiliated LPs:** The MFN does not entitle the LP to look at side letters for LPs affiliated with the GP entity (such as the fund's principals).

- **Specific Carveouts:** Many MFN provisions carve out specific rights, which are not subject to MFNs. Examples include special regulatory/tax provisions or the right to be on the LP advisory committee. This list of carveouts is often negotiated.

As mentioned above, GPs should be very careful when offering preferential side-letter terms to investors—especially smaller investors. If a big investor wants to join the fund later and insists on being granted an MFN, they may be able to swipe the special provisions you gave to earlier LPs. Beware!

⚠ FUND TRAP #9: AGREEING TO LOOSEY-GOOSEY MFNS

MFNs are very powerful. GPs should allocate them sparingly (or not at all). Early in a fund's life, GPs should be careful not to give any side-letter terms they wouldn't want a large LP with an MFN to pick up in a subsequent closing. In some cases, you might be able to "MFN-proof a side letter" by explicitly tying the side letter to some specific condition (such as being an investor at the fund's initial closing date), but you should absolutely discuss MFN strategy with your lawyer early in the process.

When granting an MFN to an investor, you should think critically about whether you've offered any tantalizing terms to other LPs. If you have, you might try to carve them out of the MFN you give to the new, large investor.

I once worked on a fund where the GP absolutely insisted on granting an MFN (with no carveouts) to an early LP with a commitment of $5 million. Granting an MFN without carveouts is always a dangerous business.

Later in the fundraise, an $8 million investor came in—they also insisted on an MFN. Because both investors had an MFN, they were each able to take all the provisions from the other's side letter. As a result, the fund had two almost identical side letters—one from each LP. This is a situation GPs should try to avoid. Use MFNs sparingly. If you do grant MFNs, make sure they have adequate carveouts.

2. Reduced Management Fees

The GP can agree to reduce (or waive entirely) the management fees an LP would otherwise pay. For example, the management fee percentage applicable to the investor could be reduced from 2 percent annually to 1 percent.

3. Reduced Carried Interest

The GP can reduce (or waive entirely) the carried interest they would otherwise receive with respect to an LP's investment. For example, the carried interest percentage applicable to an LP's investment could be reduced from 20 percent to 15 percent.

4. Co-Investment Rights

LPs love co-investment rights. The GP can grant an LP the right to invest their pro rata share (based on fund commitments) in any co-investment or follow-on investment opportunity. In some cases, an LP might get the right to co-invest with reduced (or waived) management fees and/or carried interest. We discussed co-investment rights in Chapter 6.

5. Pro Rata Rights in Future Funds

Similar to co-investment rights, an LP might gain the right to invest a certain dollar amount (or percentage of total commitments) in the sponsor's next investment fund or syndication.

6. Limited Partner Advisory Committee (LPAC)

Large or strategic LPs might ask for the right to be on the fund's LPAC, as discussed in Chapter 6. Slightly less important investors might seek the right to have a non-voting observer on the LPAC, which enables them to gather information even if they can't vote.

Sample Administrative Terms in Side Letters
1. Excluded Investments

Some LPs have a list of investments they absolutely won't invest in. If the fund invests in any of these categories, the GP will exclude the applicable LP from the investment. The following are common excluded investments:

- Drugs
- Alcohol
- Porn
- Weapons
- Cryptocurrency
- Fossil fuels
- Non-US investments

In some cases, a government investor might request to be excluded from participating in any investment outside their jurisdiction. For example, an Arizona state institution might want to be excluded from investments outside Arizona.

2. Affiliate Transfers

The general rule in most funds and syndications is that investors cannot transfer their investment in the fund to other parties without the GP's consent. In many cases, LPs ask for the right to transfer their interest in the fund to their affiliates without needing the GP's approval. This typically isn't controversial.

3. Confidentiality

Side letters can have all sorts of special confidentiality provisions. For example, a fund-of-funds investing in a fund or syndication might request the right to disclose certain information to its own underlying investors. Many LPs also request side-letter provisions preventing the GP from publicly disclosing that the LP is an investor in the fund without the LP's permission.

4. Tax and Regulatory Provisions

Many LPs (especially non-US investors, tax-exempt investors, banks, and government investors) have a cornucopia of special tax and regulatory provisions in their form side-letter requests.

MOVING NEGOTIATION REQUESTS FROM THE LPA TO A SIDE LETTER

In some cases, an LP might ask for a provision to be put in the LPA, but the GP doesn't want to change the fund documents! Maybe the fund has already held its initial closing, and the GP doesn't want to go through the headache of having the LPs approve an LPA amendment.

A common solution is to put whatever the LP asked for in a side letter. For example, an LP might ask for a cap on organizational expenses. This is something that would typically go in the LPA. However, to make the process easier, the parties might agree to put the organizational expense cap in a side letter.

TIPS FOR NEGOTIATING SPECIFIC FUND TERMS

Now that we understand the architecture for negotiating, let's look at some examples of how GPs and LPs might negotiate and provide incentives. This chapter doesn't include a comprehensive list of all negotiated terms, but it will give you a framework for how to think about GP/LP negotiations. For a refresher on what these terms mean, revisit Chapter 6.

CLASSES OF LIMITED PARTNERS

As we'll see below, sometimes GPs divide LPs into classes based on check size. For example:

- **Class A:** LPs who invest at least $1 million
- **Class B:** LPs who invest less than $1 million

Class A investors might have lower management fee percentages, lower carried interest percentages, higher preferred returns, or special information rights. We'll see some examples below. This is a great way to incentivize LPs to invest more money.

1. CARRIED INTEREST AND MANAGEMENT FEES

Tips for GPs:

- Create classes of LPs and give lower carry splits, lower management fees, and higher preferred returns to LPs who invest more money
- Avoid management fee offsets (things that reduce the management fee)
- Avoid giving LPs slices of carried interest
- Include a GP catchup in your distribution waterfall

Tips for LPs:

- Ask for lower carry splits, lower management fees, or higher preferred returns via side letters
- Ask for the management fee to go to zero once the GP starts extending the term of the fund
- Negotiate management fee offsets for excess organizational expenses, placement fees, and transaction fees
- If you're a very large LP (an anchor investor), ask for a piece of the carried interest

2. SUBSEQUENT CLOSINGS

Tips for GPs:

- Offer management fee discounts to LPs who invest on the initial closing date
- Offer other incentives to investors who join early

Tips for LPs:

- Ask the GP to waive the "catchup" interest payment if you come in after the initial closing date (I don't love this, but some funds will do it for big investors)

3. FUND EXPENSES

Tips for GPs:

- Have a broad but reasonable list of "fund expenses" payable by the fund
- Include a high cap on organizational expenses or no cap at all (you'll want to keep costs down regardless as the more you spend, the longer it will take to return capital and earn carried interest—see Chapter 7)

Tips for LPs:

- Negotiate the removal of any fund expenses that you think should be paid by the GP (examples: GP salaries, office rent, and equipment)
- Ask for a reasonable cap on organizational expenses

4. GP REMOVAL

Tips for GPs:

- Include only "for cause" removal or decline to include a GP removal provision altogether
- Require a high percentage of LPs to vote for removal (e.g., 80 percent)
- Include a narrow definition of "cause" (perhaps only fraud or willful misconduct)

- For removal "for any reason," include a grace period (e.g., you can't be removed in the first two years—you should get a fair chance to prove yourself)

Tips for LPs:

- Include "for cause" and "for any reason" GP removal
- Require a low percentage of LPs to vote for removal (e.g., a majority)
- Include a broad definition of "cause" (fraud, willful misconduct, violation of law, gross negligence, reckless conduct, etc.)

5. CO-INVESTMENTS

Tips for GPs:

- Permit the GP to allocate co-investments at their discretion
- Permit the GP to charge whatever fees/carry they want at the co-investment level

Tips for LPs:

- Include pro rata rights permitting LPs to invest in co-investments (in the same proportion as their ownership in the main fund/syndication)
- Negotiate reduced (or waived) fees/carry for any co-investments

Once all your LPs are on board, it's time for the big day—the initial closing! In the next chapter, we'll discuss how to successfully navigate this most exciting day.

CHAPTER 10

—

What Are the Mechanics for Admitting Investors into a Fund?

Time to herd the cats! In this chapter, you're going to learn how to hold your fund's initial closing. The initial closing date is a big deal for most GPs. It means you've raised capital, you've found the right deals, and you're ready to get rolling on the business of the fund.

WHEN ARE YOU READY TO CLOSE?

GPs typically decide to hold the initial closing once they have a critical mass of capital commitments. Most funds don't raise the entire fund at the initial closing. As described in Chapter 5, funds typically keep fundraising for months (or years) while making their initial investments.

Everyone is different. We've seen funds hold initial closings once they've secured anywhere from 5 to 100 percent of their target capital commitments (helpful range, huh?)—with the majority in the 10–50 percent range. First-time fund managers are usually on the lower end of that range.

The best time to hold your initial closing is as soon as you have enough commitments to start executing on the fund's strategy. On one hand, you want your investors "locked in" and committed to the fund, but on the other hand, you want to ensure you have enough commitments to make running the fund worth it for you. Additionally, you'll have bills to pay at the initial closing. Lawyers, administrators, and other service providers often defer a portion of their fees until the fund's initial closing date.

COMMITTED CAPITAL VS. CAPITAL CONTRIBUTIONS

As a refresher, "committed capital" refers to how much money your investors have promised to contribute to the fund over the fund's life. An investor's capital commitment is typically contained in their subscription agreement.

An LP's "capital contributions" are how much money the LP has actually sent to the fund.

When you hold the initial closing, each LP's commitment is locked in, and you now have the legal authority to start requesting capital contributions (to pay for deals, management fees, and other fund expenses). An LP's capital contributions cannot exceed its capital commitment.

SO...WHEN DO YOU GET THE MONEY?

Some GPs wait until they have a deal ready to close before they hold the fund's initial closing—and then they call capital immediately. Other GPs elect to hold a "dry closing"—this is where you officially hold the initial closing (where investors legally commit to the fund) but wait to call capital until you have a deal about to close. We'll discuss capital calls in detail in the next chapter.

WHAT DOCUMENTS NEED TO BE SIGNED AT CLOSING?

The key documents signed at the initial closing are:

- Each investor's subscription documents (sub docs)
- The fund's limited partnership agreement (LPA)
- Ancillary documents

We covered these documents in Chapter 8. In this section, we'll go into detail about who signs what...and when.

SUBSCRIPTION DOCUMENTS (SUB DOCS)

The initial closing officially occurs when you countersign your first investor's sub docs. Your lawyer should help with this process.

As a GP, you'll need to review each investor's sub docs to ensure they're filled out correctly (and that your LPs are qualified to invest in the fund). Best practice is for you to collect sub docs (signed by the LPs) as they come in and hold them on ice until you're ready to close. Then, you sign them all at once.

There are many software options available that make signing and reviewing sub docs easy. They cost extra money but reduce headaches considerably. You can also use DocuSign or have investors fill out PDFs, but that can get obnoxious if you have more than a few LPs. Ask your lawyer for suggestions.

You should counter-sign sub docs when you're ready to hold your fund's initial closing and not a moment before. Holding the initial closing date triggers certain regulatory filing deadlines (discussed below), so you don't want to accidentally close before you're ready.

⚠ FUND TRAP #10: SIGNING WITH GREAT ENTHUSIASM (WITHOUT TELLING YOUR LAWYER)

Despite my warning, some of you lovely GPs will sign the sub docs early and send your poor lawyers into a frenzy. As discussed below, you need to file your Form D and Blue Sky filings within fifteen days of the fund's initial closing date. If you accidentally counter-sign sub docs early (thereby holding the initial closing early), that fifteen-day clock starts ticking.

If your Blue Sky filings are submitted late, some states will impose a late fee, making an already annoying tax even harder to stomach. Don't be the client that closes a month too early without telling your lawyer! It's happened before (and I'm sure it will happen again to some nervous counselor of the law out there).

LIMITED PARTNERSHIP AGREEMENT (LPA)

Unlike the sub docs, the LPs (usually) don't sign the LPA. The GP signs the LPA on behalf of the LPs. The GP can do this because of a limited power of attorney granted by the LPs to the GP in the sub docs. As far as timing, the GP signs the LPA at the initial closing.

As a reminder from Chapter 8, the LPA signed at the initial closing is the "Amended and Restated LPA." Typically, your lawyer will prepare a very simple "initial LPA" weeks ahead of the initial closing. You can use this initial LPA to open bank accounts and sign other fund-related documents in advance of the initial closing date.

ANCILLARY DOCUMENTS

In addition to the sub docs and the LPA, there are a handful of other agreements and resolutions to sign that serve to "button up" the initial closing and ensure everything is documented correctly. We discussed these documents in Chapter 8, but here are some examples to refresh your memory:

- **Management Services Agreement:** This agreement officially "hires" the ManCo to manage the affairs of the fund.
- **Corporate Resolutions:** These are resolutions of the members of the GP authorizing it to create the fund, hire the ManCo, and admit investors into the fund.
- **Reg D-Covered Person Questionnaire:** This questionnaire helps ensure the fund or syndication is not disqualified by the SEC from selling securities under the Regulation D exemption of the Securities Act.

WHAT REGULATORY FILINGS DO YOU NEED TO MAKE?

Even though many funds are formed under exemptions to the big three securities laws, you will still need to make at least two securities filings at the initial closing. For an in-depth summary of securities laws applicable to investment funds and syndications, please see Part II.

FORM D

A Form D filing lets the SEC know you're selling securities. It must be filed within fifteen days of your initial closing (or else!). The process is a little tricky, so it's best to get started on it early. Here are the key steps:

1. **Form ID:** Submit a Form ID application to the SEC. This sets up the fund's official reporting account with the SEC. This document must be notarized and uploaded to the SEC's (notoriously finicky) website. In fact, the SEC's website also takes holidays, weekends, and nights off (ostensibly to spend time with its kids).
2. **SEC Codes:** Assuming you filed your Form ID properly, you'll receive "SEC codes" that enable you to file documents in the SEC's system as a securities issuer. Save these codes!
3. **Form D:** Fill out, sign, and submit Form D online using your SEC codes.

If you prefer, you can also pre-file your Form D before you hold your initial closing date. This is what we at our firm do for most of our clients as it reduces stress and allows funds to disclose slightly less information than if they file post-closing.

BLUE SKY FILINGS

In addition to Form D (which is a federal filing with the SEC), each state collects its own info (and fees) regarding securities you sell to investors in that state. Quite the racket. Thankfully, there is a centralized site called NASAA where you can make all the required filings and pay the fees at once. Not as exciting as rockets, but close.

Blue Sky filings must be made within fifteen days of your initial closing. Unlike Form D, you cannot pre-file Blue Sky documents in advance. In addition, you must file your Form D before using NASAA to make your Blue Sky filings. Please note that you must make Blue Sky filings in every state where your LPs are located...except Florida, which kindly does not require Blue Sky filings.

WHAT ABOUT THE INVESTMENT ADVISERS ACT?

Don't forget about the Investment Advisers Act and similar state-level rules! Here are some additional filings you may need to make depending on your fund size, asset class, and headquarters location:

- **Form ADV:** Required for registered investment advisers (RIAs).
- **Form ADV, Part 1A:** Required for exempt reporting advisers (ERAs).
- **State-Level Filings:** Required in certain cases in certain states.

Check out Chapters 14 and 15 for a comprehensive overview of these forms and when you might need to file them. Make sure to ask your lawyer about these filings.

KNOW-YOUR-CUSTOMER/ ANTI-MONEY-LAUNDERING

Lastly, you'll want to collect know-your-customer/anti-money-laundering (KYC/AML) info. Well, I don't know if you will *want* to, but you should. KYC/AML information (such as driver's licenses for individuals and formation documents for entities) helps ensure your LPs aren't on a sanctions list somewhere. Better safe than sorry!

The easiest way to collect this information is to work with a third-party administrator. Ideally, this administrator will also assist you with investor onboarding, subscription agreements, and capital calls (among other things). We discussed fund administrators in Chapter 3.

After writing the first draft of this book, the Financial Crimes Enforcement Network (FinCEN) issued a new rule under the

Bank Secrecy Act that will require RIAs and ERAs to implement seriously beefed-up KYC/AML procedures and reporting. This is a new law that will go into effect on January 1, 2026. You should ask your lawyer about this.

SUMMARY OF CLOSING CHECKLIST

In short, you'll need to do the following on your fund's initial closing date:

1. Counter-sign sub docs (LPs and GP)
2. Sign LPA and ancillary documents (GP)
3. File Form D
4. File Blue Sky filings
5. Collect KYC/AML information
6. Celebrate!

Next up, we'll learn the mechanics of calling capital from your investors once you've held the initial closing date.

CHAPTER 11

How Do You Call Capital from Investors?

Once you've officially held your fund's initial closing, it's time to get the money! In this chapter, we'll discuss the process of calling capital from investors. Please note that this chapter has a particular focus on closed-end funds and syndications. Open-end funds—especially hedge funds—often call 100 percent of LP capital and invest it immediately.

YOUR FIRST CAPITAL CALL— SHOW ME THE MONEY!

In Chapter 10, we learned how LPs "commit" capital to the fund at the initial closing date. An LP's capital commitment is the full amount of money the LP has agreed to invest in the fund or syndication. Once the first LPs officially sign the documents and commit, you can issue your first capital call notice to LPs. In this notice, you ask investors to send you money by a certain date. In many fund documents, LPs have ten business days to send the money after the GP calls capital.

An investment fund's very first capital call often includes money for the following:

- Reimbursing the fund principals for costs incurred to form and raise the fund
- Paying the first quarter's management fee
- Deploying cash to make the fund's first investment(s)
- Contributing their pro rata share of warehoused investments (discussed below)

Once you issue the first capital call, you're off to the races!

WAREHOUSED INVESTMENTS

In some cases, the GP might identify an asset they want to buy before the fund's initial closing date. The GP (or their affiliates) might (i) buy this deal themselves and sell it to the fund after the initial closing date, (ii) pre-fund capital contributions into the fund before the official initial closing, or (iii) lend money to the fund before the initial closing date to enable the fund to buy the investment.

In any of the three options above, the fund's first capital call might include funds to repay the GP (or their affiliates) for the capital contributed (or loaned) to purchase the warehoused investment.

If you're a GP with a warehoused investment, you should disclose it in your fund documents. LPs should understand the material facts, such as the price you paid and the price the fund will pay (which are often the same price). As these transactions involve conflicts of interest, you must disclose, disclose, disclose!

WHY DON'T YOU CALL 100 PERCENT OF THE CAPITAL IMMEDIATELY?

In most multi-asset funds, the GP doesn't call all the money at once. There are two (related) reasons why you don't want to call more capital than you actually need.

1. **IRR Metrics:** Internal rate of return (IRR) is a *time-based* metric. The less time you hold an investor's dollars, the better your IRR. Therefore, you don't want to call capital unless you need it for live deals or expenses.
2. **Preferred Return:** The preferred return—like IRR—is calculated based on when the LP's capital contributions enter the fund. The longer you wait to call capital, the less preferred return accrues.

In practice, the cadence of calling capital varies from fund to fund. On one hand, GPs want IRR to be as high as possible (and the preferred return to be as low as possible). On the other hand, you don't want to annoy LPs by calling capital every fifteen days just so you can optimize return metrics.

CALLING CAPITAL IN SINGLE-ASSET SYNDICATIONS

In single-asset syndications, it's common to call 100 percent of the money at once, especially for venture capital–style syndications. For some other syndications (such as real estate development), it's more common to call capital over time.

WHAT GOES IN A CAPITAL CALL NOTICE?

Two things absolutely must be in a capital call notice:

1. How much money does the LP need to send?
2. When is the due date?

Some funds might also require you to specify what the capital will be used for. LPs might request in the LPA (or a side letter) that capital call notices contain a detailed list of uses (e.g., management fees, investments, and other fund expenses).

CAPITAL CALLS ARE TYPICALLY PRO RATA

In most investment funds and syndications, capital calls are pro rata, meaning every investor puts in the same percentage of their capital commitment. For example, at the first capital call, the GP might call 20 percent of each LP's commitment. There are special circumstances (such as excused investments) where this isn't the case, but nine times out of ten, capital is called pro rata based on commitments.

WHO'S IN CHARGE OF CALLING CAPITAL?

If the fund has a third-party fund administrator (discussed in Chapter 3), they will handle calculating the capital calls, issuing capital call notices, monitoring incoming wires, and updating the fund's books and records. If the fund doesn't have a fund administrator, someone on the GP's team will be responsible for calling capital. If you have the financial capacity to hire an administrator, it's often a good idea.

WHY DO PEOPLE ON THE INTERNET SOMETIMES COMPLAIN ABOUT CAPITAL CALLS?

After reading this chapter, you should have a solid understanding of capital calls. But you might be thinking, "Why do people on social media hate capital calls and suggest 'calling capital' is a sign of a bad GP?"

TWO TYPES OF "CAPITAL CALLS"— MANDATORY VS. OPTIONAL

These disgruntled individuals are usually talking about calls for "additional capital" in syndications. Our internet friends aren't complaining about the normal fund capital calls we've discussed in this chapter. Instead, they're talking about calls for additional capital above and beyond an LP's initial commitment.

For example, someone might have a $100,000 commitment to a real estate syndication that has been fully funded. Due to economic conditions or poor execution, the syndication might be in hot water and need additional capital.

Many syndication documents have a mechanism where the GP can issue an "optional" capital call notice to raise extra money. While these capital calls are technically optional, non-funding LPs are typically diluted if they don't fund the "optional" additional contribution. Some syndication documents have punitive dilution where non-funding LPs really get whacked if they decline to wire additional funds.

So, that's why some people don't like capital calls. But now you understand that the calls they are complaining about are *not* the same as the capital calls in a multi-asset fund that draws down capital over time, which are completely normal.

WHAT HAPPENS IF AN LP INVESTS IN A FUND AFTER THE INITIAL CLOSING DATE?

As discussed in Chapter 5, most closed-end funds continue fundraising for twelve to eighteen months after the initial closing date. During that time, the fund typically invests and fundraises simultaneously.

From an accounting perspective, four main things can happen when an LP is admitted during this fundraising window after the fund's initial closing:

1. Equalization of capital contributions (mandatory)
2. Penalty interest on equalization amounts (optional)
3. Catch-up management fees (optional)
4. Interest on management fees (optional)

1. EQUALIZATION OF CAPITAL CONTRIBUTIONS

When a new LP joins a fund, the LP must contribute an amount to the fund such that after the contribution is made, each LP has contributed the same percentage of their capital commitment. Let's work through an example to see how this works in practice.

Early Emily joined the fund on the initial closing date with a capital commitment of $100, which she funded immediately. Emily's funded commitment is $100 and her unfunded commitment is $0.

Late Larry is now joining the fund one year after the initial closing date and has a capital commitment of $100. There are two general ways to handle Larry's admission. In either case, the result must be that Emily and Larry have funded the same proportion of their capital commitments.

- **Option 1:** Larry contributes 100 percent of his capital commitment ($100) to the fund and is treated as if he contributed the $100 on the initial closing date. Both Emily and Larry have contributed 100 percent of their capital commitment.

- **Option 2:** Larry contributes 50 percent of his capital commitment ($50) to the fund and is treated as if he contributed the $50 on the initial closing date. The fund then sends that $50 to Emily as a sort of refund. The $50 sent to Emily can be called again by the fund. Both Emily and Larry have contributed 50 percent of their capital commitment, and 50 percent may be called in the future.

After this equalization process, Emily and Larry are treated as complete equals going forward.

2. PENALTY INTEREST ON EQUALIZATION AMOUNTS

You might be thinking, "Why would anyone invest at the initial closing date if they can wait and see whether the fund is successful before investing?" Good question!

Most LPAs have a provision requiring late LPs to pay interest on the catch-up equalization payments ($100 in Option 1 and $50 in Option 2). GPs can choose the interest rate, but it's often somewhere around the prime rate plus 2 percent (which would be about 10 percent per annum as of this writing).

This interest is paid by the late LP (Larry in the example above) to the earlier LPs (Emily). The interest payment mechanism acknowledges the time value of money *and* the fact that the early LPs took more risks when the fund was less certain.

The GP often has the right to waive the catch-up interest payment. While this is sometimes done, I don't love this philosophically. The interest is paid to the early LPs, not the GP. In my opinion, the LPs should get the interest payments they're due. Regardless of my opinions, sometimes GPs do waive this interest. If a big LP wants to join the fund at a late closing, you might see them ask for a waiver of the catch-up interest in their side-letter request.

3. CATCH-UP MANAGEMENT FEES

In many fund agreements, late LPs must pay the GP management fees from the initial closing date (in a lump sum). The GP can typically waive these catch-up management fees at their discretion (which is much more reasonable than waiving the interest paid to LPs in my opinion).

4. INTEREST ON MANAGEMENT FEES

The GP can also theoretically charge late LPs interest on the catch-up management fees. This is usually waivable at the GP's discretion.

⚠ **FUND TRAP #11: HOLDING TOO MANY CLOSINGS**

Most funds try not to hold too many official closings. For example, a fund might have three closing dates. While you can technically hold as many closings as you want, you have to recalculate all the commitments and run the equalization process each time you hold a closing, which can get complicated. It's much simpler to deal with the closing mechanics just a few times.

I've had clients want to hold a closing each time an LP signed sub docs. However, as you've learned in this chapter, that can result in an accounting nightmare for your administrator. Better to keep your number of closings under control.

WHAT HAPPENS IF AN LP DOESN'T SEND THE MONEY?

If an LP doesn't send money after receiving a capital call notice, the LP gets in big trouble (worse than sitting alone in the corner in the red "timeout" chair). The fund documents should have a Defaulting Limited Partner section that addresses the remedies and process if an LP doesn't fund a capital call.

Here are some of the remedies available to GPs in a typical fund LPA for dealing with an LP who has defaulted:

- **Default Interest:** The GP can charge a high rate of "default" interest on the amounts the LP should have funded.
- **Suspend Distributions:** The defaulting LP cannot receive distributions until the default is cured.
- **Forced Sale:** The GP can force the LP to sell their interest to someone else. In some cases, the GP might have the right to buy out the LP at a predetermined price (e.g., 50 percent of market value).
- **Lawsuit:** The GP can sue the LP for specific performance (forcing the LP to fund their capital call).
- **The Nuclear Option:** The GP may have the right to cancel the LP's interest in the fund for no consideration and kick it out. Some LPs negotiate the removal of this option via a side letter.

WHAT DO GPS TYPICALLY DO IN REAL LIFE?

When a defaulting LP situation actually occurs, GPs are often somewhat merciful. They want to maintain a positive reputation. Examples of less draconian responses include:

- Help the LP sell their interest to someone else
- Give the LP an extension to make the capital call
- Excuse the LP from the capital call

In 2022, when people were having liquidity problems, the most common solution was helping the LP transfer their unfunded commitment to someone else. Being a GP is a long game, and you don't want to develop a reputation for being difficult or vindictive.

WHAT IF AN LP DOESN'T FUND THEIR VERY FIRST CAPITAL CALL?

The short answer is you're out of luck. While technically you can yell, complain, stamp your feet, and sue, I've never actually heard of a GP suing an LP to compel them to fund their capital call. If the LP had the money, they probably wouldn't have defaulted.

ESCROWING LP FUNDS TO MINIMIZE DEFAULT RISK

One way to mitigate default risk is to require LPs to pre-fund some or all of their commitment into an escrow account (separate from the fund's main bank account). Then, the GP calls capital from the escrow account instead of from the LPs directly.

Understandably, some LPs don't like this. The money in the escrow account doesn't accrue a preferred return or count toward IRR calculations. LPs would often rather have the money in their own high-yield savings account than a savings account controlled by the fund. In some cases, this "escrow" requirement applies only to LPs writing smaller checks. In addition to reducing default risk, this strategy incentivizes people to increase their commitments.

Alright, my friend! You've made it to the end of Part I, and you now know how to raise a fund or syndication. In Part II, you'll learn how to run your fund or syndication in compliance with securities laws and stay out of trouble.

How to Comply with Laws Governing Investment Funds

CHAPTER 12

The Securities Act of 1933

Now that you've raised your fund, you need to stay out of jail. I'm (mostly) kidding. In this part of the book, I'm going to provide an overview of key laws governing investment funds and syndications to help you stay compliant.

First up is the Securities Act of 1933. The big one! The Securities Act applies to anyone selling securities. And guess what? You're almost certainly selling securities.

WHAT IS A SECURITY?

In typically dense fashion, the Securities Act defines "security" as follows:[1]

> The term "security" means any note, stock, treasury stock, security future, security-based swap, bond, debenture, evidence of indebtedness, certificate of interest or participation in any profit-sharing

---

[1]   15 U.S. Code § 77b—Definitions; promotion of efficiency, competition, and capital formation | U.S. Code | US Law | LII / Legal Information Institute.

agreement, collateral-trust certificate, preorganization certificate or subscription, transferable share, investment contract, voting-trust certificate, certificate of deposit for a security, fractional undivided interest in oil, gas, or other mineral rights, any put, call, straddle, option, or privilege on any security, certificate of deposit, or group or index of securities (including any interest therein or based on the value thereof), or any put, call, straddle, option, or privilege entered into on a national securities exchange relating to foreign currency, or, in general, any interest or instrument commonly known as a "security", or any certificate of interest or participation in, temporary or interim certificate for, receipt for, guarantee of, or warrant or right to subscribe to or purchase, any of the foregoing.

To help refine the statutory definition, the courts have developed a couple of common tests.

THE "HOWEY TEST"

The famous Howey Test lays out the four main factors of an "investment contract" (which is a common type of security):[2]

1. An investment of money
2. In a common enterprise
3. With the expectation of profit
4. To be derived from the efforts of others

There are other tests for other types of securities, but this is the one you'll hear people talking about the most. In case you weren't sure, passive interests in funds and syndications (which

---

2   SEC v. W.J. Howey Co. | 328 U.S. 293 (1946) | Justia U.S. Supreme Court Center.

you'll sell to LPs) fit squarely within the Howey Test's definition of securities.

THE REVES TEST

The other popular test is the Reves Test, which is used to determine whether a promissory note counts as a security.[3] Feel free to go look this up in your free time, but it's not going to be directly relevant to us for the purposes of this book.

THE PRACTICAL BOTTOM LINE

I've discussed these tests for the legal nerds out there. In practice, you can safely assume that if you are soliciting passive investors (publicly or privately) to invest in your fund, syndication, or other pooled investment vehicle, you are selling securities.

On the other hand, if you are merely seeking a business partner (or to form a joint venture where both parties have significant control over the investment), you're likely not selling securities. But double check with your lawyer. Every situation is different.

WHAT MUST YOU DO IF YOU'RE SELLING SECURITIES?

As a general rule, if you are selling securities, you must either:

- **Register:** Register the securities with the SEC
- **Find an Exemption:** Sell the securities pursuant to an exemption from SEC registration

---

3   Reves v. Ernst & Young | 494 U.S. 56 (1990) | Justia U.S. Supreme Court Center.

Registering the securities means issuing an initial public offering (or other take-public transaction) for your fund or syndication. Unless you are raising an utterly massive investment vehicle, you do *not* want to go public. Way too burdensome and expensive. Too much lawyer time for your own good. You want an exemption. One hundred percent of my clients use an exemption.

WHAT EXEMPTIONS FROM SECURITIES REGISTRATION ARE THERE?

Common exemptions to SEC registration include:

- **Regulation A:** A public/private hybrid that has two tiers (Tier 1 for simpler raises of up to $20 million in a twelve-month period, and Tier 2 for more complex raises of up to $75 million in a twelve-month period). Regulation A requires significant disclosure and process.
- **Regulation S:** An exemption for sales of securities outside the US.
- **Regulation CF:** The "crowdfunding" exemption that allows you to raise up to $5 million in a twelve-month period. It has investment limits and other technical requirements.
- **4(a)(2):** An exemption for transactions by an issuer of securities not involving a public offering.

While these exemptions are all well and good, they're too expensive, complicated, or uncertain for most investment funds and syndications. Instead, most GPs turn to the golden child: Regulation D.

REGULATION D

Regulation D is a magnificent law that provides a "safe harbor" for certain securities offerings. There are multiple flavors to Regulation D. The two most typical options for investment funds and syndications are Rule 506(b) and Rule 506(c). They're easy to use, do not limit the amount of money you can raise, and require less lawyer time (and money) than the other options, so long as each investor you accept is an accredited investor.[4]

WHAT IS AN ACCREDITED INVESTOR?

There are many ways to be accredited, but the most common are:

- **Individual (Income):** An individual with $200,000 in annual income (or $300,000 joint income with a spouse) for the last two years with an expectation to continue earning income above the threshold.
- **Individual (Net Worth):** An individual with a $1 million net worth (excluding the value of the primary residence and any debt thereon).
- **Individual (Tests):** An individual with certain securities licenses (such as Series 7, Series 65, or Series 82).
- **Entity (Assets):** An entity with at least $5 million in assets.
- **Entity (All Owners Accredited):** An entity where each of the equity owners is an accredited investor.

Also, if you're the GP of a fund or syndication, you're an accredited investor with respect to that particular fund or syndication. Your fund's sub docs will have a full list of options for

---

4   17 CFR § 230.506—Exemption for limited offers and sales without regard to dollar amount of offering. | Electronic Code of Federal Regulations (e-CFR) | US Law | LII / Legal Information Institute.

becoming an accredited investor for LPs to choose from. For more options, check out the SEC's website.[5] Alright, now that we understand what makes an investor accredited, let's evaluate 506(b) and 506(c) in detail.

RULE 506(B)—"506 BE QUIET!"

506(b) is a great option for the true "private placement" of securities. This is the version of fundraising most people are used to.

Advantages of 506(b)

The beauty of 506(b) is you can have investors self-certify whether they're an accredited investor in their sub docs. All you have to do is ask (assuming you don't have reason to believe they're lying). This is very simple and low friction.

Disadvantages of 506(b)

You must have a preexisting relationship with each investor. Friends, family, etc. In other words, you have to know all your LPs *before* they invest. To use 506(b), you cannot fundraise in the following ways:

- Podcasts
- Twitter (or X, if I must)
- LinkedIn
- Advertisements
- Fund-related speeches at conferences
- Blasting an email to a bunch of people you don't know

---

5   SEC.gov I Accredited Investors.

- Running around Times Square with a sandwich board

Basically, you can't talk about your fund in public. So...what can you talk about?

In general, it's best to avoid any mention of the fund or fundraising. You can potentially offer your views on the market but don't solicit investors or even suggest you're raising money. It's a gray, murky analysis. I counsel clients that it's better to be safe than sorry and advise erring on the side of saying less rather than more. When in doubt, ask your lawyer.

⚠ FUND TRAP #12: ACCEPTING NON-ACCREDITED INVESTORS IN A 506(B) OFFERING

506(b) technically allows you to have up to thirty-five nonaccredited investors. Many lawyers will tell you that. What many lawyers forget is that, pursuant to Section 502(b), if you accept *even one* nonaccredited investor, you must do a bunch of extra disclosure. I was considering listing the full cornucopia of requirements here but decided to save a forest.

Basically, if you accept a nonaccredited investor, you need a mountain of disclosure, similar to what you would need to disclose if you were using Regulation A. For this reason, many funds accept only accredited investors even if they use Rule 506(b). Please read this section again if you're planning to use 506(b). Lawyers routinely *don't* know this part of the law and put their clients at risk.

At a previous firm, we had a client who absolutely insisted he wanted to accept non-accredited investors (against our advice). He ended up spending five figures and untold hours on the additional disclosure. It's just not worth it for the vast majority of GPs.

RULE 506(C)—"COME SEE OUR FUND!"

506(c) is a newer creature (born in 2013) that is becoming increasingly popular. It allows for the public solicitation of investors.

Advantages of 506(c)

506(c) is great because you don't need to worry about what you say in public. Go ahead and talk about your fund or syndication wherever you want. You can post about fundraising on the internet. You can go on podcasts. You can even advertise (though I'll leave it to you to decide whether you think that's a good idea from a reputational perspective).

Disadvantages of 506(c)

Unlike 506(b), you must "take reasonable steps to verify" that 100 percent of your investors are accredited. You can do this by getting a letter from each investor's attorney, CPA, or financial advisor verifying accreditation. You can also hire a third party to verify investors for you. Several online services will do this for around $50. Not bad at all. In a pinch, you can also review investor tax returns to verify income.

Just before this book was finalized by the publisher, the SEC issued a "no action letter" suggesting that a GP could assume that investors are accredited if the following requirements are met:

- **Minimum Investment:** The minimum check size is $200k for individuals and $1 million for entities.
- **LP Representations:** The LP represents that it is not financing any portion of its capital commitment.

- **GP Representations:** The GP represents that it isn't aware of any untrue statements of fact by the LP regarding its accredited status.

If the LP is an entity that is accredited only because all of the LPs' owners are accredited, then each of the above applies to each of the LP's underlying equity owners.

For larger funds with larger minimums, this may offer an easy way to use 506(c) without explicit third-party verification. Ask your lawyer!

WHICH IS BETTER—506(B) OR (C)?

In short, the benefit of 506(c) is you can raise money publicly. The benefit of 506(b) is investors can self-certify that they are accredited without meeting the new minimum check size thresholds.

If you're not sure which you prefer, you can switch from 506(b) to 506(c) if you change your mind mid-fundraise. However, you cannot go from 506(c) back to 506(b). No putting the genie back in the bottle, toothpaste back in the tube, rabbit back in the hat, etc. You're locked in.

Most of your legal documents will be the same whether you use 506(b) or 506(c). The only real difference will be that you should make it clear in 506(c) subscription documents that each investor absolutely must be accredited. You can also include a form accredited-investor-verification letter the investor can send to their financial professional.

WHAT GOVERNMENT FILINGS ARE
REQUIRED FOR REGULATION D?

If you use either 506(b) or 506(c), you must file a Form D with the SEC no later than fifteen days after the fund's initial closing date. You'll also need to make state-level Blue Sky filings. We discussed these filings in detail in Chapter 10. They're not that bad.

BAD ACTOR DISQUALIFICATION

506(b) and 506(c) are *not* available to "bad actors," as set forth in 506(d). Examples of "bad acts" include being convicted of financial crimes, being barred from being a financial professional, and generally getting into trouble with the SEC.

If you have been subject to one of these "disqualifying events," prohibiting you from using Regulation D, you can still sell securities—it's just more difficult. If you can't use Regulation D, one common route is to use 4(a)(2). However, unlike Regulation D, 4(a)(2) doesn't "preempt" state law.

If you use Regulation D, you generally don't need to deal with state-specific versions of the Securities Act (other than making Blue Sky filings). If you use 4(a)(2), you need to research and comply with the state-specific version of the Securities Act in each state where one of your investors is based. Regulation D is much easier to work with than 4(a)(2).

NO BAMBOOZLING THE PUBLIC

No matter how you sell securities, Regulation D or otherwise, you can't lie. More specifically, Rule 10b-5 of the Securities Exchange Act prohibits fraud, material misstatements and/or omissions, and other methods of deceit in connection with the sale or purchase of securities. Court cases have held that private citizens (as well as the SEC) can go after issuers of securities (including fund managers) for these actions, which are generally referred to as securities fraud.

Please, don't commit fraud. You should have your lawyer review all your marketing materials (such as your marketing deck and PPM) to ensure you aren't overpromising or misrepresenting anything. And, for the love of funds, never "guarantee" returns.

Next up, we're going to review the second big law governing investment funds and syndications: the Investment Company Act.

CHAPTER 13

The Investment Company Act of 1940

In the last chapter, we discussed the Securities Act, which applies to essentially all investment funds and syndications. In this chapter, you'll learn about the Investment Company Act.

WHO DOES THE INVESTMENT COMPANY ACT APPLY TO?

The Investment Company Act applies to investment companies (big surprise). The statutory definition of "investment company" according to Title 15 of the US Code is as follows:[6]

---

6   15 U.S. Code § 80a–3—Definition of investment company | U.S. Code | US Law | LII / Legal Information Institute.

(a) Definitions

(1) When used in this subchapter, "investment company" means any issuer which—

(A) is or holds itself out as being engaged primarily, or proposes to engage primarily, in the business of investing, reinvesting, or trading in securities;

(B) is engaged or proposes to engage in the business of issuing face-amount certificates of the installment type, or has been engaged in such business and has any such certificate outstanding; or

(C) is engaged or proposes to engage in the business of investing, reinvesting, owning, holding, or trading in securities, and owns or proposes to acquire investment securities having a value exceeding 40 per centum of the value of such issuer's total assets (exclusive of Government securities and cash items) on an unconsolidated basis.

(2) As used in this section, "investment securities" includes all securities except (A) Government securities, (B) securities issued by employees' securities companies, and (C) securities issued by majority-owned subsidiaries of the owner which (i) are not investment companies, and (ii) are not relying on the exception from the definition of investment company in paragraph (1) or (7) of subsection (c).

In short, the two main ways to become classified as an investment company are:

- **Primarily Investing in Securities:** The business is primarily engaged in investing in securities (or holds itself out as being primarily engaged in investing in securities).
- **40 Percent Asset Test:** Even if the business isn't "primarily" investing in securities, it can be considered an investment company if at least 40 percent of the business's assets are securities (excluding government securities).

Private equity funds, venture capital funds, and hedge funds are typical examples of investment companies.

WHAT ABOUT REAL ESTATE FUNDS AND SYNDICATIONS?

Real estate (buildings, land, etc.) is not a security. As a result, pure real estate funds and syndications are typically not considered investment companies and do not need to deal with the Investment Company Act.

However, a real estate fund-of-funds *does* invest in securities (i.e., the securities of the underlying fund) and would typically be considered an investment company. A fund formed to invest in passive joint-venture interests may also be considered an investment company. Determining classification under the Investment Company Act involves a case-by-case analysis of the facts of each particular situation. Check with your lawyer!

WHAT ABOUT DEBT FUNDS AND SYNDICATIONS?

Under the Securities Act (discussed in Chapter 12), many debt instruments are not securities. However, it's generally understood that most debt instruments *are* securities for the purposes of the Investment Company Act and the Investment Advisers Act (discussed in Chapter 14).

Counterintuitively, many debt funds are considered investment companies even though the funds themselves might not be investing in things considered securities under the Securities Act. Again, this will involve a case-by-case analysis by your lawyer.

WHAT HAPPENS IF YOU'RE AN INVESTMENT COMPANY?

Investment companies without an exemption are subject to significant SEC regulation. These non-exempt investment companies—such as mutual funds and exchange-traded funds (ETFs)—are often referred to as "40 Act" funds.

Lots of lawyer time and legal bills (and headaches) are required to manage and maintain 40 Act funds. Most small and medium-sized funds and syndications can't support the weight of these regulations. Luckily, there are several statutory exemptions from registering as a 40 Act fund.

The most common exemptions for private funds and syndications are:

- 3(c)(1): The "100 Investor" exemption
- 3(c)(7): The "Qualified Purchaser" exemption
- 3(c)(5)(C): The "Real Estate" exemption

Let's examine each in turn.

3(C)(1)—THE "100 INVESTOR" EXEMPTION

One way to be exempt from the onerous 40 Act requirements is to limit your fund or syndication to one hundred investors or fewer. Simple enough? Not so fast. Counting is harder than you might think! Some investors count as more than one investor. The rules are complicated enough that we can't get into them all here, but here are some examples:

- **Newly-Formed LLC:** If people form an LLC just to invest in your fund or syndication, you may need to count all the owners of that LLC.
- **Fund-of-Funds:** If a fund-of-funds is more than 10 percent of your fund's equity, you may need to count all the fund-of-funds' investors.
- **40 Percent Test:** If more than 40 percent of an entity's assets are invested in your fund/syndication, you may need to count all the entity's investors.

Your investment fund's sub docs should include questions for your investors regarding 3(c)(1) "investor counting." Your lawyer will help you review investors' answers to ensure you have a good 3(c)(1) exemption from the Investment Company Act.

⚠ FUND TRAP #13: ACCEPTING SMALL INVESTORS WHO FILL UP YOUR 3(C)(1) SLOTS

Early in the fundraising process, GPs often take whatever money they can get. Twenty-five thousand dollars here. Fifty thousand dollars there. It's understandable. They want to get the ball rolling. (I once saw an LP try to invest $2,000.)

However, 3(c)(1) funds should be careful about accepting smaller checks, especially when the investing entities count as more than one investor for 3(c)(1) purposes. For example, you might have a potential LP that wants to invest $100,000—your fund's minimum. However, the potential LP is an LLC newly formed by eight friends to invest in your fund. If admitted, the LLC would take up eight slots for 3(c)(1) purposes—contributing just $12,500 per slot. Is it worth admitting them?

I've seen this happen to fund managers before: they were overzealous about accepting as much money as possible and then ran into their one-hundred-investor cap sooner than expected. Your lawyer should explicitly let you know when any investor would count as more than one for 3(c)(1) purposes. Then, you can make the judgment call as to whether the LP is worth admitting.

NOTE ON SMALL VENTURE CAPITAL FUNDS

Venture capital funds have special 3(c)(1) thresholds. If the fund has less than $12 million in commitments (recently raised from $10 million), the fund can have up to 250 investors. There have also been political rumblings about increasing these thresholds even further. The venture capital lobby must be powerful (see Chapter 14 for more on this). I'll leave it to you to decide for yourself whether you would want to run a $12 million fund with 250 investors.

3(C)(7)—THE "QUALIFIED PURCHASER" EXEMPTION

An investment company can also be exempt from the Investment Company Act if 100 percent of its investors (other than members of the GP team) are "qualified purchasers" (i.e., really fancy people). The bar to becoming a qualified purchaser is much higher than the accredited investor threshold. Generally, individuals must have investment assets of at least $5 million and entities must have investment assets of at least $25 million to be considered a qualified purchaser.

KNOWLEDGEABLE EMPLOYEES

You may have noticed that "other than members of the GP team" language up there. What's that about? Well, the GP and their core team (called "knowledgeable employees") can invest in a 3(c)(7) fund even if they aren't qualified purchasers. The Code of Federal Regulations (CFR) states the following:[7]

> *(b) For purposes of determining the number of beneficial owners of a Section 3(c)(1) Company, and whether the outstanding securities of a Section 3(c)(7) Company are owned exclusively by qualified purchasers, there shall be excluded securities beneficially owned by:*
>
> > *(1) A person who at the time such securities were acquired was a Knowledgeable Employee of such Company;*
> >
> > *(2) A company owned exclusively by Knowledgeable Employees;*
> >
> > *(3) Any person who acquires securities originally acquired by a Knowledgeable Employee in accordance with this section, provided that such securities were acquired by such person in accordance with § 270.3c-6*

Note that only high-level employees count. Lower-level staff who are not part of the investment decision-making process are not considered knowledgeable employees. See the text from the CFR below:[8]

---

7   17 CFR § 270.3c-5—Beneficial ownership by knowledgeable employees and certain other persons. | Electronic Code of Federal Regulations (e-CFR) | US Law | LII / Legal Information Institute.

8   17 CFR § 270.3c-5—Beneficial ownership by knowledgeable employees and certain other persons. | Electronic Code of Federal Regulations (e-CFR) | US Law | LII / Legal Information Institute.

(4) The term Knowledgeable Employee with respect to any Covered Company means any natural person who is:

(i) An Executive Officer, director, trustee, general partner, advisory board member, or person serving in a similar capacity, of the Covered Company or an Affiliated Management Person of the Covered Company; or

(ii) An employee of the Covered Company or an Affiliated Management Person of the Covered Company (other than an employee performing solely clerical, secretarial or administrative functions with regard to such company or its investments) who, in connection with his or her regular functions or duties, participates in the investment activities of such Covered Company, other Covered Companies, or investment companies the investment activities of which are managed by such Affiliated Management Person of the Covered Company, provided that such employee has been performing such functions and duties for or on behalf of the Covered Company or the Affiliated Management Person of the Covered Company, or substantially similar functions or duties for or on behalf of another company for at least 12 months.

By the way, knowledgeable employees are also excluded from the one-hundred-investor limit in 3(c)(1).

PARALLEL FUNDS

Does a cap of one hundred investors seem too restrictive? Upset that you have some investors who are not qualified purchasers? There's gotta be a better way! Well, there's a solution: parallel funds.

Parallel funds are side-by-side 3(c)(1) and 3(c)(7) funds. You fill one fund with no more than one hundred investors and the other with only qualified purchasers. Then, when you invest in underlying assets, each fund contributes a portion of the capital required. In some cases, you can form an "aggregator" entity jointly owned by the 3(c)(1) fund and the 3(c)(7) fund. It goes without saying that you should work with a lawyer if you want to raise parallel funds (but I said it anyway).

3(C)(5)(C)—THE "REAL ESTATE" EXEMPTION

One last exemption to discuss! We learned above that pure real estate funds are often outside the reach of the Investment Company Act. But...what if you're a real estate debt fund? What if some of your assets are real estate equity and some are real estate debt? What if some of your assets are passive interests in other funds, syndications, or joint ventures?

Then, you need 3(c)(5)(C), which exempts funds "purchasing or otherwise acquiring mortgages and other liens on and interest in real estate."[9] To rely on 3(c)(5)(C), the fund must meet the following requirements:[10]

1. At least 55 percent of the fund's assets must consist of "qualifying investments." A qualifying investment is an actual interest in real estate or a loan/lien fully secured by real estate.
2. At least 80 percent of the fund's assets must consist of qualifying assets or "real estate-type interests."

---

9   15 U.S. Code § 80a–3—Definition of investment company | U.S. Code | US Law | LII / Legal Information Institute.

10   https://www.sec.gov/divisions/investment/noaction/2017/redwood-group-101617.htm?utm_source=www.fundamentals.law&utm_medium=referral&utm_campaign=3-key-fund-spv-laws-you-must-know-part-2#_ftn3.

3. No more than 20 percent of the fund's total assets can consist of assets that have no relationship to real estate.

As usual, this is something to talk to your lawyer about. The analysis can get tricky.

NOTE ON OPEN-END FUNDS

3(c)(5)(C) is not available to funds "in the business of issuing redeemable securities."[11] "Redeemable securities" are defined in Title 15 of the US Code as follows:[12]

"Redeemable security" means any security, other than short-term paper, under the terms of which the holder, upon its presentation to the issuer or to a person designated by the issuer, is entitled (whether absolutely or only out of surplus) to receive approximately his proportionate share of the issuer's current net assets, or the cash equivalent thereof.

Financial products like mutual funds and ETFs are typically redeemable securities—it's very easy to sell shares in an ETF. Interests in typical hedge funds with easy liquidity are also likely redeemable securities. However, there's some gray area around whether open-end real estate–related funds issue redeemable securities. In fact, two of the big law firms I've worked at have disagreed on this point!

In general, the more restrictions imposed on LP withdrawals/ redemptions, the less likely it is the fund will be deemed to have

---

11   15 U.S. Code § 80a–3—Definition of investment company I U.S. Code I US Law I LII / Legal Information Institute.

12   15 U.S. Code § 80a–2—Definitions; applicability; rulemaking considerations I U.S. Code I US Law I LII / Legal Information Institute.

redeemable securities. If you need to rely on 3(c)(5)(C), you may want to make LP redemptions at the GP's discretion (or require several conditions on withdrawal to be satisfied before redeeming). Check out Chapter 5 for a discussion on lockups and gates to manage liquidity and withdrawals.

NOTE ON 3(C)(5)(C) VS. 3(C)(1) AND 3(C)(7)

If you have the choice of relying on 3(c)(1), 3(c)(7), or 3(c)(5)(C), you may want to choose 3(c)(5)(C). If recently killed private fund rules (implemented by the SEC and struck down by the Fifth Circuit Court of Appeals) were revived, many of the new regulations would apply to 3(c)(1) funds and 3(c)(7) funds but not 3(c)(5)(C) funds. Perhaps the SEC will give up and not try to revive these comprehensive reforms. But you never know.

Similarly, the new FinCEN KYC/AML rules mentioned in Chapter 10 will apply to 3(c)(1) funds and 3(c)(7) funds but do not look like they'll apply to 3(c)(5)(C) funds. If you can avoid investing in real estate "securities" (and stick to pure dirt and buildings), it may make your life easier from a regulatory perspective.

Next up, we'll discuss the Investment Company Act's fraternal twin—the Investment Advisers Act.

CHAPTER 14

The Investment Advisers
Act of 1940

In this chapter, we'll discuss the third in the big trifecta of laws governing investment funds and syndications: the Investment Advisers Act of 1940. The Investment Advisers Act applies to (shockingly) investment advisers.

DEFINITION OF "INVESTMENT ADVISER"

The Investment Advisers Act defines "investment adviser" as follows:[13]

> Any person who, for compensation, engages in the business of advising others, either directly or through publications or writings, as to the value of securities or as to the advisability of investing in, purchasing, or selling securities, or who, for compensation and as

---

13   15 U.S. Code § 80b-2—Definitions | U.S. Code | US Law | LII / Legal Information Institute.

part of a regular business, issues or promulgates analyses or reports concerning securities.

In short, an investment adviser is a person (or entity) engaged in the business of advising others as to the value of securities for compensation. Let's parse the language in this definition a bit.

"ENGAGES IN THE BUSINESS"

The SEC interprets this broadly. You're likely considered "engaged in the business" of investment advising if you:

- Hold yourself out as an investment adviser, financial planner, or similar
- Charge a fee for investment advice
- Provide advice regularly

"ADVISING OTHERS...AS TO THE VALUE OF SECURITIES"

Examples of "advice" include recommendations regarding:

- Stocks, bonds, mutual funds, and interests in limited partnerships
- Market trends and asset allocation
- Investment manager selection
- Market valuations and security lists

If you're not advising clients on "securities," then you might not be considered an investment adviser. In the context of investment fund managers, the following asset classes are generally subject to the Investment Advisers Act:

- Private equity
- Venture capital
- Hedge funds
- Funds-of-funds
- Debt funds

Real estate isn't a security, so if you invest in pure real estate (dirt and buildings), you typically would not be subject to the Investment Advisers Act (but see the discussion from the last chapter on real estate–related securities, which *would* bring you under the jurisdiction of the Investment Advisers Act).

"FOR COMPENSATION"

Compensation includes any economic benefit received for giving advice, such as advisory fees, commissions, fees for total services rendered, and other similar payments.

STATUTORY EXCLUSIONS

There are several statutory exceptions to the definition of "investment adviser," including:[14]

- **Banks:** Regulated banks
- **Professionals:** Any lawyer, accountant, engineer, or teacher whose advice regarding securities is merely incidental to the practice of their professional services
- **Brokers:** Any broker or dealer whose advice regarding securities is merely incidental to the practice of their professional

---

14   15 U.S. Code § 80b-2—Definitions | U.S. Code | US Law | LII / Legal Information Institute.

services and who receives no special compensation for the advice

- **Publications:** News publications with a general and regular circulation
- **Treasuries:** Advice regarding securities of the US government
- **Credit Rating Agencies:** Moody's, Fitch, S&P, etc.
- **Family Offices:** Family offices (as defined by the SEC)

These statutory exclusions aren't much help for investment fund managers, but luckily, there are a few special exemptions tailormade for investment funds. Very convenient!

THREE KEY EXEMPTIONS TO THE INVESTMENT ADVISERS ACT FOR INVESTMENT FUND MANAGERS

To avoid registering as an RIA (discussed below), investment fund managers typically seek an exemption from registration. Here, we'll hit the three main exemptions available to fund managers.

PRIVATE FUND EXEMPTION (RULE 203(M)-1)

The private fund exemption applies to investment fund managers with less than $150 million of regulatory assets under management.

Calculating Regulatory Assets Under Management

"Regulatory assets under management" is calculated on a gross, fair-market-value basis across all your securities portfolios, including:

- Investment portfolios where at least 50 percent of the portfolio consists of securities
- All private funds (funds exempt under 3(c)(1) or 3(c)(7)—discussed in Chapter 13)
- Family and proprietary accounts
- Accounts for which you receive no compensation for your services

Note that "regulatory assets under management" is your total assets under management across all these portfolios, not the assets under management of any particular fund. Form ADV has a helpful section on calculating regulatory assets under management. Search Form ADV for "Instructions for Part 1A" and go to Item 5(b).

VENTURE CAPITAL EXEMPTION (RULE 203(L)-1)

I suppose the venture capital lobby is good at its job because there's a specific exemption for venture capital funds. To be an exempt venture capital fund, the fund must (among other requirements) comply with the following conditions from the CFR:[15]

(1) Represents to investors and potential investors that it pursues a venture capital strategy;

(2) Immediately after the acquisition of any asset, other than qualifying investments or short-term holdings, holds no more than 20 percent of the amount of the fund's aggregate capital contributions

---

15   17 CFR § 275.203(l)-1—Venture capital fund defined. | Electronic Code of Federal Regulations (e-CFR) | US Law | LII / Legal Information Institute.

and uncalled committed capital in assets (other than short-term holdings) that are not qualifying investments, valued at cost or fair value, consistently applied by the fund; and

(3) Does not borrow, issue debt obligations, provide guarantees or otherwise incur leverage, in excess of 15 percent of the private fund's aggregate capital contributions and uncalled committed capital, and any such borrowing, indebtedness, guarantee or leverage is for a non-renewable term of no longer than 120 calendar days, except that any guarantee by the private fund of a qualifying portfolio company's obligations up to the amount of the value of the private fund's investment in the qualifying portfolio company is not subject to the 120 calendar day limit.

Let's review each requirement in detail.

Prong 1: Venture Capital Strategy

Venture capital funds typically include a sentence saying they are pursuing a venture capital strategy in the PPM, LPA, and other governing documents. Simple enough.

Prong 2: No More Than 20 Percent Non-Qualifying Investments

No more than 20 percent of the fund's assets can be invested in assets that are not "qualifying investments." Qualifying investments include equity securities acquired directly from a qualifying portfolio company, which is a company that satisfies *each* of the following criteria:

- **No Public Companies:** At the time of the fund's investment, is a private company

- **No Leveraged Buyouts:** Does not borrow or issue debt in connection with the fund's investment and distribute the borrowing proceeds to the fund
- **No Fund Investments:** Is not an investment company, private fund, or commodity pool; it should be a real operating business selling goods or services

In short, "qualifying investments" are directly acquired equity securities of operating businesses.

What About Secondaries?

Secondaries are not "acquired directly" from a qualifying portfolio company and are thus not qualifying investments. Therefore, for a fund to fall under the venture capital exemption, secondaries can sometimes be a risky business. The fund can invest in secondaries but must ensure at least 80 percent of its assets are non-secondary qualifying investments. If you're a venture capitalist, please read the previous paragraph twice. Maybe three times.

Prong 3: 15 Percent Leverage Limit

The fund cannot have debt in excess of 15 percent of the total fund size. In addition, the debt cannot have a term of more than 120 days (subject to some exceptions). In practice, venture funds don't often use debt, other than "subscription lines" that enable the fund to borrow cash to fund short-term needs without calling capital from investors. The fund may use a subscription line to make an investment quickly, avoid annoying LPs with too many capital calls, or, less virtuously, juice IRR.

⚠ FUND TRAP #14: BLOWING YOUR "VENTURE CAPITAL" EXEMPTION

Per the SEC, "an adviser is eligible to rely on the venture capital exemption only if it solely advises venture capital funds."[16] In other words, you can't use the venture capital exemption if you manage venture capital funds alongside private equity funds, hedge funds, or secondaries funds. We touched on this in Chapter 4, but it's so important that I wanted to highlight it again.

More than once, I've seen managers who thought they were exempt, but they actually had some secondaries funds, which blew their entire venture capital exemption. When this happens, the manager might sell their secondaries investments to get back into compliance. However, this process can get messy and fraught with conflict. It's much better to set things up the right way from the beginning so don't become a forced seller.

By the way, a similar thing happens to real estate investors who start investing in debt, preferred equity, and other security-like positions. GPs often mistakenly believe they're exempt when they're not. Work with your lawyer to ensure you don't accidentally subject yourself to provisions of the Investment Advisers Act you'd rather avoid.

FOREIGN PRIVATE ADVISER EXEMPTION (RULE 202(A)(30)-1)

A non-US adviser may be exempt if they satisfy all the following criteria:[17]

---

16 Final Rule: Exemptions for Advisers to Venture Capital Funds, Private Fund Advisers With Less Than $150 Million in Assets Under Management, and Foreign Private Advisers.

17 17 CFR 275.202(a)(30)-1—Foreign private advisers.

- **Limited US Nexus:** No place of business in the United States and does not hold themselves out to the US public as an investment adviser
- **Limited US Clients:** Has fewer than fifteen clients and private fund investors in the United States
- **Limited US Assets Under Management:** Has less than $25 million of regulatory assets under management attributable to US clients and investors (see Calculating Regulatory Assets Under Management, above)

For the second bullet in the above list, "counting" US private fund investors is similar to counting under 3(c)(1) of the Investment Company Act. We discussed counting in Chapter 13.

SELECTING EXEMPTIONS

As long as you fit within one of the exemptions above, you're generally good. Emerging managers can often rely on the private fund exception (less than $150 million in assets under management) for quite a while. However, they should always look to the future to determine what exemptions (if any) they might be able to use once they cross the $150 million threshold. In some cases, managers might alter their investment strategy to avoid registration.

For example, a venture capital fund could decline to purchase secondaries so it can stay within the venture capital exemption. Or, a real estate fund might avoid investing in other real estate funds or syndications to escape the Investment Advisers Act altogether.

BECOMING A REGISTERED INVESTMENT ADVISER (RIA)

If you cross the $150 million assets under management threshold and can't find another exemption you qualify for, you must register with the SEC as an RIA. Here, we'll briefly discuss the regulatory and compliance requirements applicable to RIAs.

FORM ADV

To register as an RIA, you need to file Form ADV electronically via the Investment Adviser Registration Depository (IARD).

Form ADV Part 1 collects basic information about the investment adviser, such as identity, number of employees, regulatory assets under management, and information about clients, managed funds, and key personnel (including criminal/disciplinary history).

Form ADV Part 2 contains more-specific disclosures about the investment adviser's business, such as information on key personnel, fees and compensation arrangements, methods of analysis, strategy, risks, code of ethics, financial industry affiliations, brokerage/custody arrangements, and various other financial details.

How Do You Prepare Form ADV?

You will want help from a lawyer or compliance consultant to file Form ADV. Compliance consultants are firms that specialize in RIA compliance matters. They will often prepare your Form ADV at a lower cost than a lawyer. In any case, you'll need a lot of input from your team to prepare Form ADV. It's a relatively large undertaking.

Annual Form ADV Updates

RIAs must file an updated Form ADV every year within ninety days of the end of their fiscal year. There's often a mad dash in early spring to get ADVs filed. I would suggest preparing early. Your lawyer or compliance consultant will be grateful.

ADDITIONAL REQUIREMENTS FOR RIAS

In addition to filing and maintaining Form ADV, RIAs are subject to various additional compliance measures, including:

- **Custody Rule:** RIAs must maintain client funds with a qualified custodian, provide various statements to clients, and submit to unannounced audits.
- **Marketing Rule:** RIAs are subject to strict rules regarding advertising and marketing, including mandatory disclosure of performance results, testimonials, and endorsements.
- **Chief Compliance Officer:** RIAs must appoint a Chief Compliance Officer responsible for the RIA's compliance with regulations, including conducting an annual review, training, education, monitoring, testing, and reporting.

DO INVESTMENT MANAGERS WANT TO BECOME RIAS?

Due to the increased regulatory burden, most investment fund managers try to avoid registration as long as possible. However, a minority of managers submit to registration voluntarily. Their goal is to increase credibility with sophisticated investors. They make a cost-benefit calculation that the increased compliance requirements are worth it. Investment managers are permitted to register as an RIA once they have $100 million in regulatory assets under management (or once they would be required to register with fifteen or more states).

EXEMPT REPORTING ADVISER (ERA) FILING

Investment fund managers with at least $25 million in assets under management but who are exempt from registering as RIAs are called Exempt Reporting Advisers (ERAs).

While ERAs aren't subject to nearly the same regulatory burden as RIAs, they still must file Part 1A of Form ADV with the SEC within sixty days of crossing the $25 million threshold. Like RIAs, ERAs must update their Form ADV each year.

NOTE ON THE (DEAD) PRIVATE FUND RULES

Last year, the SEC adopted a huge package of new rules applicable to private investment funds that included new audit requirements, side-letter restrictions, quarterly statement rules, prohibited activities, and a few other matters.

It was a whole big thing we investment fund nerds spent a lot of time learning about. Then, out of nowhere, the Fifth Circuit Court of Appeals torpedoed the whole slate of rules in *National Association of Private Fund Managers v. Securities and Exchange Commission.*

It's possible the SEC will appeal, but as of right now, the rules are not happening. While some lawyers are likely weeping in their offices singing "How Could This Happen to Me?," it's a big win for investment managers.

WHAT ABOUT STATE LAW?

This whole chapter has been about federal regulation of investment advisers. However, many fund managers (especially emerging managers and managers who are not RIAs) are also subject to state investment adviser laws. We'll discuss state laws in the next chapter.

CHAPTER 15

State Investment Adviser Laws

As mentioned in the last chapter, investment fund managers must deal with state laws if they aren't RIAs with the SEC.

Pursuant to the National Securities Markets Improvement Act of 1996, the federal Investment Advisers Act "preempts" state law once an investment adviser registers with the SEC as an RIA. In other words, once a fund manager is a full-blown RIA, they generally no longer need to deal with state investment adviser laws.

In short: investment fund managers are subject to state investment adviser laws unless and until they become RIAs.

Even fund managers relying on the exemptions from registration we discussed in Chapter 14 are subject to these state laws, including those using the private fund exemption (less than $150 million in assets under management) and the exemption for venture capital fund managers.

If you're an emerging fund manager (outside certain asset classes like real estate), you likely need to comply with state investment adviser laws. Each state has its own laws. And the states vary wildly on how strict their rules are.

THE NASAA MODEL RULE

Many states have adopted a model rule (or a variation thereof) developed by the North American Securities Administrators Association (NASAA—the same group that helped you transmit Blue Sky filings in Chapter 10). This rule includes registration requirements and exemptions similar to the federal laws we discussed in Chapter 14.

GENERAL REGISTRATION EXEMPTIONS

First, to have a good exemption, there are some generally applicable requirements:

Under the NASAA model rule, private fund advisers can avoid registration with the state if they meet the following requirements:[18]

(1) neither the private fund adviser nor any of its advisory affiliates are subject to an event that would disqualify an issuer under Rule 506(d)(1) of SEC Regulation D, 17 C.F.R. §230.506(d)(1);

(2) the private fund adviser files with the state each report and amendment thereto that an exempt reporting adviser is required to file with the Securities and Exchange Commission pursuant to SEC Rule 204-4, 17 C.F.R. § 275.204-4; and

(3) the private fund adviser pays the fees specified in Section XXX [410 of USA 2002].

In short:

---

18   NASAA-Registration-Exemption-for-Investment-Advisers-to-Private-Funds-Model-Rule-
     Amended-Oct.-8-2013.pdf

- **Bad Actor:** The adviser cannot be subject to a "bad actor disqualification"—we discussed this in Chapter 12.
- **ERA Filing:** The adviser must make an ERA filing with their home state—we discussed ERA filings in Chapter 14.
- **Fee:** As usual, someone wants a fee.

ADDITIONAL REQUIREMENTS FOR 3(C)(1) FUNDS THAT ARE NOT VENTURE CAPITAL FUNDS

If the adviser has any funds (other than venture capital funds) that rely on 3(c)(1) of the Investment Company Act, they must meet the following additional requirements:[19]

(1) The private fund adviser shall advise only those 3(c)(1) funds (other than venture capital funds) whose outstanding securities (other than short-term paper) are beneficially owned entirely by persons who, after deducting the value of the primary residence from the person's net worth, would each meet the definition of a qualified client in SEC Rule 205-3, 17 C.F.R. § 275.205-3, at the time the securities are purchased from the issuer;

(2) At the time of purchase, the private fund adviser shall disclose the following in writing to each beneficial owner of a 3(c)(1) fund that is not a venture capital fund:

(A) all services, if any, to be provided to individual beneficial owners;

---

19 NASAA-Registration-Exemption-for-Investment-Advisers-to-Private-Funds-Model-Rule-Amended-Oct.-8-2013.pdf.

(B) all duties, if any, the investment adviser owes to the beneficial owners; and

(C) any other material information affecting the rights or responsibilities of the beneficial owners.

(3) The private fund adviser shall obtain on an annual basis audited financial statements of each 3(c)(1) fund that is not a venture capital fund, and shall deliver a copy of such audited financial statements to each beneficial owner of the fund.

In short:

- **Qualified Clients:** The adviser cannot accept investors in any non-venture capital 3(c)(1) fund unless the investors are qualified clients—generally people who have a net worth of $2.2 million or invest at least $1.1 million with the investment adviser.
- **Information:** The adviser must provide certain information to investors at the time of investment.
- **Audit:** Each non-venture capital 3(c)(1) fund must have an annual audit and present the results to investors.

If all the adviser's funds are 3(c)(7) funds, all the adviser's funds are venture capital funds, or all the adviser's funds are outside the Investment Company Act's purview altogether, the adviser would not typically need to comply with these extra rules. Check out Chapter 13 to learn more about 3(c)(1) and 3(c)(7) funds.

⚠ FUND TRAP #15: RAISING A SMALL FUND BEFORE CONSIDERING STATE INVESTMENT ADVISER LAWS

These requirements—especially the "qualified client" and the "audit" provisions—can be quite burdensome for small funds. In fact, small managers seeking to raise a few million dollars may ultimately decline to raise a fund in certain states because the audit requirement is too burdensome or their investor base wouldn't consist entirely of qualified clients.

The bottom line is that the NASAA model rule isn't that bad for venture capital managers or managers who don't need to rely on 3(c)(1). However, for those non-venture capital managers who do need 3(c)(1), the model rule can be a serious roadblock.

More than once, I've talked to small private equity fund managers who need to have their financial statements audited to become compliant. They shrivel in despair when they calculate the fee drag an audit will cause on their small fund. Please, please, please, ask your lawyer about these laws before forming a fund.

SUMMARY OF INVESTMENT ADVISER LAWS IN ALL FIFTY STATES AND WASHINGTON, DC

Now that we understand the NASAA model rule, let's categorize each of the fifty states into a few buckets. Ultimately, you 100 percent want to work with a lawyer when starting a fund or syndication. This list is just a starting point, and the laws may have changed since this book was published. Alabama and Florida each changed their laws between the first draft of this book and the final version you're reading today.

If you go to fundamentals.law (our newsletter), you'll find an article titled "How to Comply with State Investment Advisers

Laws," where we have links to the investment adviser laws for each of the fifty states.

CATEGORY 1: PERMISSIVE

These states are generally quite adviser-friendly. Their rules and requirements for advisers are less burdensome than the NASAA model rule. These states have easy exemptions so long as the total number of "clients" (typically, each fund or syndication is a client) stays below a certain threshold.

- Connecticut: Unlike the NASAA model rule, Connecticut has a "private fund" exemption for managers with less than $150 million in assets under management.
- DC: Unlike the NASAA model rule, Washington, DC, has a "private fund" exemption for managers with less than $150 million in assets under management.
- Florida: Investment managers are exempt from state registration if they have less than six funds/syndications within a twelve-month period. Florida also just added a separate exemption for private fund advisers.
- Georgia: Investment managers are exempt from state registration if they have less than six funds/syndications within a twelve-month period.
- Illinois: Investment managers are exempt from state registration if they have less than five funds/syndications within a twelve-month period.
- Indiana: Investment managers are exempt from state registration if they have less than five funds/syndications within a twelve-month period and a few extra requirements.
- Kansas: Investment managers are exempt from state registration if they have less than fifteen funds/syndications.

- Louisiana: Investment managers are exempt from state registration if they have less than fifteen funds/syndications within a twelve-month period.
- New Jersey: Investment managers are exempt from state registration if they have less than fifteen funds/syndications within a twelve-month period.
- New York: Investment managers are exempt from state registration if they have less than six funds/syndications within a twelve-month period.
- North Carolina: Investment managers are exempt from state registration if they have less than fifteen funds/syndications within a twelve-month period.
- Ohio: Investment managers are exempt from state registration if they have less than fifteen funds/syndications within a twelve-month period.
- Pennsylvania: Investment managers are exempt from state registration if they have less than five funds/syndications within a twelve-month period.
- South Dakota: Exemptions mirror the federal SEC exemptions.
- Tennessee: Investment managers are exempt from state registration if they have less than fifteen funds/syndications within a twelve-month period.

CATEGORY 2: NASAA MODEL RULE

These states adopted the NASAA model rule:

- Alabama
- Colorado
- Iowa
- Massachusetts

- Minnesota
- Nevada
- New Mexico
- Rhode Island
- Virginia
- Wyoming

CATEGORY 3: NASAA MODEL RULE WITH MODIFICATIONS

These states started with the NASAA model rule but tweaked things a bit. You'll definitely want to check the particulars with your attorney.

- Arizona: Modifications making it more permissive than the NASAA model rule.
- California: Broader venture capital exemption than the NASAA model rule.
- Maine: Only minor modifications.
- Maryland: Only minor modifications.
- Michigan: Audit not required if all investors are qualified clients.
- Missouri: Certain types of accredited investors can be admitted in non-venture capital 3(c)(1) funds even if they are not qualified clients.
- Nebraska: Modifications making it slightly more permissive than the NASAA model rule.
- Oklahoma: Added the $150 million private fund exemption but removed the venture capital exemption.
- South Carolina: Various modifications, some more and some less restrictive.

- Texas: Modifications making it slightly more permissive than the NASAA model rule.
- Vermont: Only minor modifications.
- Wisconsin: In addition to the model rule, Wis. Stat. § 551.403(2)(a)(2m) provides another exemption for advisers whose only clients in Wisconsin are certain categories of accredited investors under federal Regulation D (including entities with total assets in excess of $5 million).

CATEGORY 4: BAD NEWS

These states are more restrictive than the NASAA model rule. In many cases, there are no exemptions whatsoever, meaning an investment adviser must formally register with the state (similar to registering with the SEC as an RIA) no matter what.

- Alaska: No exemptions.
- Arkansas: No exemptions.
- Delaware: Exemption only applies to 3(c)(7) funds.
- Hawaii: No exemptions.
- Idaho: No exemptions.
- Kentucky: Exemption only applies to 3(c)(7) funds.
- Montana: No exemptions.
- New Hampshire: No exemptions.
- North Dakota: No exemptions.
- Utah: Complex provision that is more restrictive than the NASAA model rule.
- Washington: Exemption only applies to 3(c)(7) funds and venture capital funds—not 3(c)(1) funds.
- West Virginia: No exemptions.

CATEGORY 5: OREGON

Oregon exempts "any person who conducts no public advertising or general solicitation in this state and whose only clients in this state are accredited investors."[20] The question is whether using 506(c) (discussed in Chapter 12) would blow this exemption. I haven't seen any guidance on this yet. 506(b) appears to be safe. Oregon always needs to do something just a little unusual. Stay weird, my friends.

Next up, the final "real" chapter of this book, where you'll learn the basics of investment fund tax law.

---

20 Or. Admin. Code § 441-175-0030—Exclusion from Definition of "Investment Adviser."

CHAPTER 16

Tax Laws (and How to Structure Around Them)

You're in the home stretch! In this chapter, we're going to discuss everyone's favorite topic...taxes! The upside of prudent tax planning is simple: both GPs and LPs get to keep more money without getting into trouble with the taxing authorities.

This chapter was co-authored by Adam Krotman, an excellent tax lawyer who our firm works with on many funds and syndications.

WHY DO INVESTMENT FUNDS INVEST IN TAX STRUCTURING?

The four main tax-related goals of GPs and LPs include the following:

1. **Minimize Taxable Income:** Not all "income" is taxable (e.g., gain on the sale of "qualified small business stock" may not be taxable). Plus, not all costs are immediately tax-

deductible—see the section on separating the GP and the ManCo below.

2. **Minimize Tax Rates:** Different types of income are taxed at different rates (e.g., carried interest income may be taxed at preferential long-term capital gain rates, while management fees are taxed as ordinary income).

3. **Defer Taxes as Long as Possible:** You are generally better off deferring taxes into later years—time value of money and all that. Plus, if you defer long enough, you may avoid the tax altogether, and your heirs might receive a stepped-up basis down the line.

4. **Tax Risk and Administration:** You'll need to determine the balance that's right for you between minimizing taxes, minimizing audit risk, and maintaining a reasonable budget for your CPA and tax lawyer.

WHICH TAXES ARE APPLICABLE TO INVESTMENT FUNDS AND SYNDICATIONS?

There are three main categories of taxes that may impact your fund's tax structure. The main concern for US-based funds and syndications is US federal income tax, but some other taxes also merit discussion.

US Federal Income Tax

As of this writing, the current top marginal tax rate for US individuals on ordinary income is a whopping 37 percent (currently scheduled to increase to 39.6 percent in 2026...we'll see what Trump does). The top marginal tax rate for US corporations is 21 percent. Finally, the top marginal tax rate for long-term capital gains and qualified dividends is effectively 23.8 percent.

Ordinary income includes most people's compensation, such as salaries and wages, and most businesses' operating income. For GPs, management fees are typically taxed at ordinary income tax rates. For LPs, income taxes affect certain types of income a fund may generate, such as interest from debt securities or hedge fund income from sales of securities held less than a year (technically, this is "short-term capital gain," which is generally taxed at the same rate as ordinary income).

Long-term capital gains include sales of assets held for investment that satisfy certain holding periods and other requirements. For funds, this often includes the sale of portfolio company equity or real estate assets held longer than a year (however, for the GP's carried interest, the holding period requirement for long-term capital gains treatment is three years).

As a super-bonus for venture capital (and some private equity) funds, portfolio company equity held for more than five years may be eligible for the "qualified small business stock" (QSBS) exemption, under which up to $10 million of gain (sometimes even more!) *per investor* (and possibly *per principal*) from the sale of the equity may be *100 percent exempt* from US federal income tax.

US State and Local Taxes

State and local tax rules often mostly mimic the federal tax rules, and planning for these taxes typically takes a backseat to planning for the US federal income tax. However, they can be substantial in certain jurisdictions and impact structure.

For example, special New York City tax rules drive many New York City-based principals to form one entity to receive the management fee and another to receive the carried interest. The application of state and local taxes usually depends on where the fund management team operates, investors reside, and/or portfolio assets are located.

Ex-US Taxes

Funds with GPs or LPs who reside and/or operate abroad or portfolio assets located offshore should be extra careful about ex-US taxes. Additionally, some funds with special structuring may have one or more entities formed in an offshore jurisdiction, such as the Cayman Islands, in which case tax planning is needed to minimize taxes in these offshore jurisdictions.

WHAT DETERMINES INVESTMENT FUND TAX STRUCTURE?

Four factors play a big role in determining the tax classifications and jurisdictions of the various entities in your fund's structure.

Fund Type and Strategy

Tax treatment and structure differ substantially across different types of funds, such as venture capital, real estate, private equity, and hedge funds. Key considerations include the anticipated asset mix, asset holding periods, income stream sources, and nature and geographic situs of fund management-team activity.

LP Base

Different "tax types" of investors are taxed differently and therefore have different tax structuring needs. Common investor tax types include:

- High net worth US taxable individuals and family offices
- Institutional US-taxable investors, such as corporate venture arms
- US tax-exempt investors, such as IRAs, private pension funds, and endowments
- "Super" tax-exempts, such as state and local government agencies and instrumentalities, including public pension funds
- Non-US investors, such as non-US individuals and sovereign wealth funds

Assets Under Management

Tax structures vary significantly in complexity, cost, and administrative burden. The right structure for a $10 million loan-origination fund may differ dramatically from a $1 billion fund in the same asset class.

Risk Tolerance

Given their complexity and uncertainty, taxes can be viewed as another type of business risk to manage. A good tax practitioner will help tailor the tax structure to the risk tolerance of the GP and LPs.

TAX TREATMENT OPTIONS

Now, let's discuss the "tax treatment" you might choose for each legal entity in your fund's structure. But first, let's clear something up. Tax structuring can get confusing because sometimes an entity's "legal" type is different from its "tax" type.

For example, an entity formed as a Delaware LLC may be classified for US federal income tax purposes as a partnership, a disregarded entity, a C-corporation, or an S-corporation! For some non-tax entities, the tax entity classification is elective. For others, it's mandatory.

Examples of forms you can use to change the tax classification of entities include Form 8832 (general tax election form) and Form 2553 (electing S-corporation status).

PASS-THROUGH ENTITIES (FOR TAX PURPOSES)

Pass-throughs include partnerships, disregarded entities, and S-corporations. Most pass-through entities in fund structures are "partnerships" or "disregarded entities." Let's look at two key characteristics of pass-through entities.

Single-Level Taxation (i.e., No Double Taxation)

Pass-through entities generally *do not pay tax at the entity level*—rather, the income or loss "earned" at the entity level "passes through" to the entity's owners and is allocated among them according to their ownership interest. For a fund, this is a complex allocation based on the investor's and principal's rights to distributions (i.e., the "distribution waterfall" discussed in Chapter 7).

Entities taxed as partnerships send K-1s to their "partners" each year detailing their allocable tax items. Then, the partners integrate these K-1s into their personal tax returns. Depending on the information in the K-1, the partners might pay tax on allocable income/gain or reduce taxable income using allocable losses.

Character and Activity Pass-Through

Pass-throughs can "pass through" the character of income, gain, or loss to their owners (including long-term capital gains, dividends, and QSBS). The activity of a pass-through can also attribute to its owners—this can be especially important for non-US investors. In short, this could cause non-US investors to be treated as engaged in a US trade or business and may force them to file a US tax return (rarely a welcome task).

Boo! Beware of "Phantom Income"

Phantom income is a spooky business. In a particular year, a pass-through entity might earn income it does not actually distribute to the partners. In this case, the owners may owe taxes on this "phantom income" without receiving cash to pay it.

Phantom income can arise for a number of reasons, including reinvestment of earnings, the establishment of reserves, or circumstances that produce taxable income without any liquid cash (e.g., deemed interest on certain debt instruments). In many cases, funds include special tax distribution provisions to help avoid this unpleasant result (discussed further below).

C-CORPORATIONS (FOR TAX PURPOSES)

Alright, let's move on to C-corporations.

Double Taxation

The big downside to C-corporations is "double taxation." First, the C-corporation may owe taxes at the entity level. The current top marginal US federal income tax rate on C-corporations is 21 percent. Next, a second level of tax may apply to the

C-corporation's equity owners when they receive distributions or sell their equity in the C-corporation.

Character and Activity Blockers

Character and activities generally do not pass through to C-corporation owners. Ordinary and capital gains income is taxed at the same C-corporation tax rate, and activities like US trade or business activity are "blocked" from attribution to non-US owners, which is why C-corporations are sometimes referred to as "blockers" in fund tax world.

US funds and syndication don't use C-corporation entities nearly as often as pass-throughs. However, C-corporations may be helpful in certain special scenarios, such as in "blocker" tax structures to accommodate non-US and/or US tax-exempt investors.

US VS. NON-US ENTITY TYPES

Pass-through entities and C-corporations may be US or non-US entities. Countries generally have different flavors of each.

In general, US entities are cheaper and easier to form and administer than most non-US entities. For that reason, the US (and Delaware in particular) is a popular jurisdiction for funds and syndications.

However, in some scenarios, tax savings may lead funds to set up non-US entities (taxed as pass-throughs or C-corporations depending on the circumstances).

A TYPICAL TAX STRUCTURE FOR
AN INVESTMENT FUND

A simple fund with US-based GPs, LPs, and investments might look something like the following graphic. For reference, the following might be for a real estate fund or syndication (which is why there's a property company to hold real estate).

Basic Fund Structure

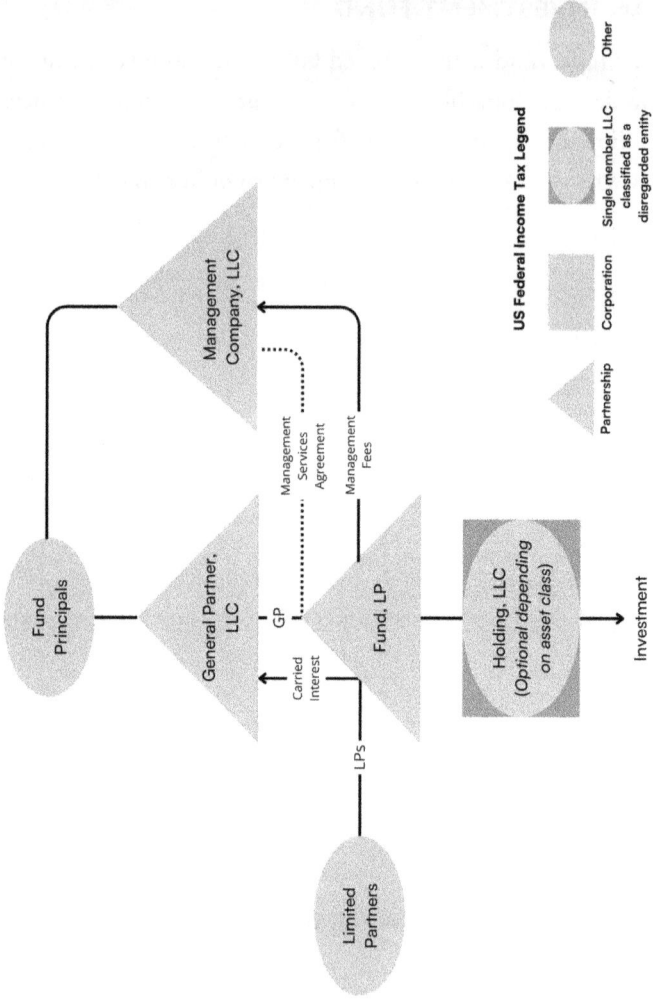

Fund Principals

Management Company, LLC

General Partner, LLC

GP

Management Services Agreement

Management Fees

Fund, LP

Carried Interest

LPs

Limited Partners

Holding, LLC
(Optional depending on asset class)

Investment

US Federal Income Tax Legend

Partnership

Corporation

Single member LLC classified as a disregarded entity

Other

In this structure, the fund, GP, and ManCo are all "pass-through" entities for US federal income tax purposes, which avoids double taxation and passes through the character of any underlying income taxed at preferential rates, such as long-term capital gain or QSBS, to the ultimate owners.

Let's examine each entity in our structure in detail.

FUND, LP (PASS-THROUGH)

Investors invest in the fund, which in turn invests in portfolio assets directly or through other subsidiary entities. In this example, the fund invests in real estate through a wholly owned LLC (taxed as a pass-through entity). The fund's principals also hold an equity interest in the fund indirectly through the GP.

The fund is the entity that directly earns taxable income from portfolio assets and incurs tax expenses, such as the management fee. The fund entity pays no fund-level taxes itself and instead allocates tax items of income or loss to the LPs and GP each year in rough parity to their respective distribution rights. Gains and losses will show up on the K-1s issued after the end of each year.

The "type" and amount of income or loss will vary significantly among different fund types and over the life cycle of a fund. For example, high-frequency hedge funds tend to generate large amounts of short-term capital gain and loss each year. On the other hand, venture capital funds often generate losses for several years and then (hopefully!) long-term capital gains or QSBS when they exit portfolio companies.

Some funds, such as venture capital funds, are highly limited in the ability of GPs or LPs to use tax losses, which are often permanently disallowed under current law. Others, such as hedge funds and real estate development funds, provide more flexibility to utilize tax losses. This feature relates to special rules that limit taxpayers' ability to use investment-related expenses and may change in 2026, when certain provisions of the 2017 tax act (TCJA) are set to expire. Different funds are treated differently under these rules depending on whether they are deemed engaged in mere passive investment or a "trade or business" for tax purposes.

GENERAL PARTNER, LLC (PASS-THROUGH)

The general partner (GP) is the entity through which the principals hold an equity interest in the fund. GPs have both a capital interest (received for the principals' investments in the fund) and a carried interest (the GP's extra share of the profits for managing the fund) in the fund.

Like the fund, the GP's pass-through nature means the GP itself pays no tax. Instead, they pass through the income or loss (and related character) to the principals.

Structuring the carried interest as an equity interest in the fund is the "magic" mechanism by which principals convert the carried interest from what would be ordinary income if received via a contractual fee for services into potential capital gains or other tax-preferred income.

To accomplish this objective, the carried interest must be carefully structured so that, among other things, (1) it is an interest only in the future profits of the fund (after a return of capital) and (2) certain three-year holding-period requirements are met for the underlying asset generating the income.

A failure to satisfy the above conditions can have catastrophic results for the principals, including potential "phantom income" taxed at ordinary income rates at the time the carried interest is granted (or vests). This can happen if the carried interest is determined not to be a so-called "profits interest" for US federal income tax purposes. Make sure to work with a good tax lawyer so this doesn't happen!

MANAGEMENT COMPANY, LLC (PASS-THROUGH)

The management company (ManCo) is often owned by the same people who own the GP. Rather than an equity interest in the fund, the ManCo typically has a management agreement with the fund requiring the fund to pay the ManCo a periodic fee for its investment-management services.

The ManCo typically employs the investment team and incurs expenses that are not allocated to the fund. Examples include salaries, office rent, and other overhead.

Just like the fund and GP, the ManCo pays no tax at the entity level and passes through income and loss to its owners. However, the ManCo owners don't get preferential long-term capital gains treatment—the fee income earned by the ManCo (management fee, other fund fees, and possibly portfolio company fees) is generally taxed at ordinary income rates.

On the other hand, unlike fund expenses (which have significant restrictions on deductibility), ManCo expenses, like salaries, professional service fees, and overhead, are typically deductible against fee income. As a result, many fund managers can limit (or even eliminate) net tax from the ManCo.

THE TAX REASONS TO SEPARATE
THE GP FROM THE MANCO

It's often preferable from a tax perspective to split up the Manco and the GP for at least three (and sometimes four) reasons:

1. **Deductibility of Expenses:** Separating the entities mitigates

the risk that ManCo-related expenses get commingled with GP expenses and/or allocated to the GP's equity interest in the fund. Such a misallocation of expenses to the GP equity interest could delay or entirely disallow the utilization of certain expenses that would normally offset ManCo fee income as it is earned. In short, misallocation could create excess tax liability and possibly "phantom" income, where owners have a tax liability without the net cash to pay the taxes.

2. **Employee Matters:** Separating the entities facilitates grants of carry equity from the GP to ManCo employees without causing the employees to lose their ManCo W-2 status and related access to certain fringe benefits.

3. **Future Planning:** Separating the entities can facilitate future tax planning in connection with potential third-party investments, insider sales, and other changes in entity ownership.

4. **State or Local Tax:** Certain state and local jurisdictions have special tax regimes that drive GPs and ManCos apart. For example, funds with New York City–based principals often divide Manco and the GP into separate entities to mitigate the impact of the dreaded New York City "unincorporated business tax," which can impose an extra 4 percent on income or gain.

Aside from tax matters, fund managers also split up the GP and ManCo to segregate assets and liabilities. As discussed in Chapter 2, the ManCo typically lasts forever, while a new GP is formed for each new fund.

SPECIAL CONSIDERATIONS FOR TAX-EXEMPT INVESTORS

The US tax code exempts certain entities from US federal income taxes (and for some, allows donors to deduct the value of their monetary contributions). These entities are broadly referred to as "US tax-exempts" or "tax-exempts" and include charities, foundations, IRAs, private pension funds, and university endowments.

Investment funds often target tax-exempt LPs. Many tax-exempts supplement their donor contributions and grants with investment income. Some also like writing big checks to funds.

WHAT IS UBTI?

But tax-exempt LPs must be careful—not all passive investment income is exempt from taxation. While rules vary, most tax-exempt LPs are subject to US federal income tax on "unrelated business taxable income," or "UBTI," which they must report on their tax returns.

In extreme cases, too much UBTI can cause certain tax-exempts to lose their tax-exempt status, which would be disastrous for the tax-exempt LP (and not great for any donors planning to deduct charitable contributions).

MOM, WHERE DOES UBTI COME FROM?

On a high level, income or gain is UBTI if it is earned from:

1. A trade or business
2. Regularly carried on
3. That is not substantially related to the tax-exempt investor's purpose

For example, let's say a tax-exempt hospital runs a bakery open to the public. The income from that bakery is likely UBTI since it's unrelated to the hospital's primary mission (taking care of patients). The hospital would have to pay taxes on all bakery income, reducing its net proceeds.

There's a laundry list of carveouts to UBTI, such as certain rental income, royalties, dividends, and capital gains. UBTI flows up to tax-exempt LPs from entities taxed as pass-throughs but is "blocked" by entities taxed as C-corporations. The use of leverage (debt) to acquire an investment (or the use of leverage by a pass-through entity owned by a tax-exempt) can convert income or gain from non-UBTI to UBTI.

GENERATING UBTI IN INVESTMENT FUNDS

For investment funds, UBTI issues arise in three common contexts:

1. **Fund-Level Trade or Business:** The fund is directly engaged in a "trade or business," such as loan origination in a private credit fund. This can be the case if the fund is originating loans and taking an origination fee.
2. **Pass-Through Portfolio Company Trade or Business:** The fund makes an equity investment in a pass-through entity (like an LLC taxed as a partnership) that is engaged in a trade or business. This is less common in venture capital (where companies are typically taxed as C-corporations) and more common in lower-middle-market private equity.
3. **Leverage:** The fund uses leverage, or a portfolio company taxed as a pass-through entity uses leverage.

Needless to say, the UBTI rules are as complex as the range of structures and mechanisms to mitigate their impact.

NINETY-NINE PROBLEMS BUT UBTI DOESN'T NEED TO BE ONE

Investment funds often try to solve UBTI problems for their investors. One common mechanism is to "block" UBTI by creating an entity taxed as an S-corporation through which the tax-exempt LP invests in the fund. You can also put the blocker elsewhere in the fund structure so long as it blocks the tax-exempt's exposure to the UBTI.

But beware—the blocker entity incurs US corporate federal income tax (currently, a 21 percent rate), and care should be taken not to expose other investors (or the carried interest!) to this tax drag. To accomplish this, your lawyer might set up parallel funds, feeder funds, or alternative investment vehicles (AIVs). The cost to set up the special structuring for the tax-exempt investors is often borne by the tax-exempt investors themselves, though some funds opt to spread the expenses across the entire (taxable and tax-exempt) LP base.

Note that the usual UBTI regime does not apply to so-called "super tax-exempts" (US governmental entities like public pension funds), which are subject to a different US tax regime and beyond the scope of this book.

Each investment fund should consult its tax advisor about whether the fund is expected to generate UBTI for tax-exempts and if so, tax planning options to address UBTI concerns.

HOW TO HANDLE UBTI CONVERSATIONS WITH LPS

In practice, GPs have three options for how to deal with UBTI situations:

1. **Do Nothing:** Some managers—especially smaller funds and syndications—disclose the UBTI risks to investors and do not undertake special structuring to mitigate UBTI issues. In these cases, tax-exempt LPs can decide whether they're willing to bear the tax drag UBTI creates or do their own structuring.

2. **Special Structuring:** Some managers—usually of larger funds with more tax-exempt investors—may choose to implement a blocker structure to accommodate tax-exempt investors or engage in other more exotic structuring. This can benefit the tax-exempt investors but requires more legal fees, entity formation, and complexity on the part of the GP.

3. **Avoid UBTI in the First Place:** Some funds, especially venture capital funds, will require all companies to convert to C-corporations before the fund will invest. Among other reasons, this helps eliminate the UBTI concerns for tax-exempt investors.

Sometimes, GPs and tax-exempt LPs do the math and conclude that generating some UBTI is preferable to the expense (e.g., US corporate income tax in a blocker structure) and/or opportunity costs of special structuring or the avoidance of UBTI-producing investments.

In some cases, large LPs might ask for a UBTI covenant. This may require the GP to take "commercially reasonable efforts" (or some other level of efforts) to mitigate UBTI concerns for tax-exempt investors. If you're a GP that agrees to a UBTI covenant, you'll need to proactively limit UBTI for your investors.

This is often a nice carrot to offer tax-exempt LPs to entice them to invest.

SPECIAL CONSIDERATIONS FOR NON-US INVESTORS

Non-US investors are an increasingly common source of capital. Many funds target Asia, Europe, Latin America, and the Middle East. When raising money offshore, you may want to contact local counsel in the countries where your investors will be. They can help with any securities laws concerns and required filings in offshore jurisdictions. This isn't a tax point, but it seemed like a good time for a reminder.

Now, on to income effectively connected with a US trade or business, or effectively connected income (ECI).

PASSIVE VS. ACTIVE INCOME (ECI)

Income earned by funds can be roughly split into two buckets for US federal income tax purposes: passive and active. Passive income includes stuff like interest, dividends, royalties, rent, and capital gains. Active income (a.k.a. "ECI") is essentially operating income from a US business. This is an oversimplification—determining whether income is "passive" or "active" (ECI) involves many nuances and exceptions in practice. But it's a helpful starting point.

For example, if a foreign entity operates a US-based manufacturing plant, income generated from that plant would count as "active" income. On the other hand, if a non-US person makes a loan to a US-based manufacturing company bearing 10 percent annual interest and owns no equity in the company, the interest is likely exempt passive income.

HOW ARE PASSIVE AND ACTIVE INCOME
TAXED FOR NON-US INVESTORS?

The "passive" regime generally applies a flat tax withholding rate on the gross amount of "US-source" passive income—the 2025 default rate is 30 percent unless a special rate or exemption applies. Two common exceptions to this withholding tax include capital gains when a fund sells equity in its portfolio companies and interest income (if the fund is not a loan-origination fund).

By contrast, the "active" (ECI) regime taxes non-US investors on net income (gross income minus expenses) at the same marginal rates that would apply to US individuals or corporations (plus, for non-US corporations, an extra "branch profits" tax to approximate the 30 percent gross withholding tax on dividends that would apply if a US corporation distributed its earnings to a non-US person).

In the tax world, this "active" type of income is typically referred to as "income effectively connected to a US trade or business," or "ECI," and non-US investors usually don't like it for reasons we will explain below!

WHY DO NON-US INVESTORS AVOID ECI?

Like UBTI for tax-exempt investors, non-US investors are often averse to earning ECI. Earning ECI can be "bad" for three main reasons:

1. **Tax Returns:** ECI triggers special US tax-return filing requirements for non-US investors. Most offshore investors don't love the requirement to file taxes in a new country.
2. **Investment Returns:** The high effective tax rates on ECI (44+ percent on non-US corporate investors) plus applicable US state and local taxes drive down investment returns.

3. **Compliance:** ECI creates additional compliance, administration, and tax liability for investment funds and syndications that have associated tax reporting and withholding obligations and may need to engage in special tax structuring.

Note that the usual ECI regime does not apply to sovereign wealth funds, which are subject to a different US tax regime and beyond the scope of this book (maybe we can talk about it in the next edition).

FIRPTA—THE SPECIAL TAX APPLICABLE TO NON-US INVESTORS IN REAL ESTATE

If you invest in real estate, read this section twice. Then read it again.

Special rules under the Foreign Investment in Real Property Tax Act (FIRPTA), enacted in 1980, classify gains from the sale or disposition of "US real property interests" (USRPIs) as a special category of ECI. Without FIRPTA, these gains would typically be exempt as "passive" income. With FIRPTA, they are generally taxed the same as ECI.

USRPIs include land, buildings, and corporations whose assets consist of 50 percent or more of USRPIs (this calculation is quite complex and, many would argue, over-inclusive!). One notable exception to FIRPTA are interests held solely as a creditor, which includes many real estate loans.

FIRPTA is bad news for similar reasons that ECI generally is bad news (see above)—it taxes income that would otherwise be exempt from US tax at ECI rates, can impose US tax-return filing requirements on the non-US investor in the year FIRPTA gain is recognized, and imposes withholding tax obligations on certain fund or portfolio entities.

GENERATING ECI IN INVESTMENT FUNDS

For investment funds, ECI issues can arise in three common contexts:

1. **Fund-Level Trade or Business:** The fund is directly engaged in a "trade or business," such as loan origination in a private credit fund. In this case, all interest, fees, and gain from the originated loans may be ECI.
2. **Pass-Through Portfolio Company Trade or Business:** The fund makes an equity investment in a pass-through entity (like an LLC taxed as a partnership) that is engaged in a US trade or business. This is less common in venture capital (where companies are typically taxed as C-corporations) and more common in lower-middle-market private equity.
3. **US Real Estate:** The fund has an ownership interest in US real estate or US companies with enough assets that the IRS treats as real property.

You may notice that, aside from US real estate, this list is eerily similar to the list of UBTI-generating activities discussed above.

HOW TO VALIANTLY PROTECT LPS FROM THE TERRORS OF ECI

Like tax-exempts and UBTI, using a "blocker" (an entity taxed as a US C-corporation) is one common mechanism to block attribution of ECI up to the non-US investor but at the cost of US corporate tax at the blocker level. The UBTI section above discussed this strategy.

However, unlike tax-exempts and UBTI, using blockers to manage ECI has an additional tax wrinkle to manage—in addition to the US corporate tax at the blocker level, distributions of funds from the blocker up to the non-US investors must be structured carefully to mitigate or avoid another level of "passive income" withholding tax on dividends. There are a range of techniques that can be utilized that are beyond the scope of this book, such as adjusting the timing of distributions, selling blocker equity in lieu of receiving blocker distributions, and capitalizing blockers with a combination of equity and debt since the return of debt principal is not typically taxable.

Blockers for non-US investors in real estate funds face additional structural challenges avoiding FIRPTA-generated ECI from certain blocker distributions or gain on the sale of their blocker interest, which may require more special structuring, such as creating one or more offshore vehicles in jurisdictions like the Cayman Islands, British Virgin Islands, or Luxembourg.

As with UBTI and tax-exempts, each investment fund should consult its tax advisor about whether the fund is expected to generate ECI for non-US investors and if so, tax planning options to address ECI concerns.

HOW TO HANDLE ECI CONVERSATIONS WITH LPS

Like with UBTI, GPs have three options for dealing with ECI situations.

1. **Do Nothing:** Some managers—especially smaller funds and syndications—disclose the ECI risks to investors and do not undertake special structuring to mitigate ECI issues. In these cases, non-US LPs can decide whether they're willing to deal with ECI or do their own structuring.
2. **Special Structuring:** Some managers—larger funds with more non-US investors—may choose to implement a blocker or

other special structure to accommodate non-US investors. This can benefit the non-US investors but requires more legal fees, entity formation, and complexity on the part of the GP.

3. **Avoid ECI in the First Place:** Some funds, especially venture capital funds, will require all companies to convert to C-corporations before the fund will invest. Among other reasons, this helps eliminate the ECI concerns for non-US investors. Of course, if you're a real estate fund, "avoid real estate" isn't really a viable option, so you'll likely need to choose options one or two above.

Sometimes, GPs and non-US LPs do the math and conclude that generating some ECI is preferable to the expense (e.g., US corporate income tax in a blocker structure) and/or opportunity costs of special structuring or the avoidance of ECI-producing investments.

In some cases, large LPs might ask for an ECI covenant. This may require the GP to take "commercially reasonable efforts" (or some other level of efforts) to mitigate ECI concerns for non-US investors. If you're a GP that agrees to an ECI covenant, you'll need to proactively limit ECI for your investors. This is often a nice carrot to offer non-US LPs to entice them to invest (and some will insist).

⚠ FUND TRAP #16: ADMITTING NON-US INVESTORS INTO A REAL ESTATE FUND WITHOUT SPECIAL STRUCTURING

Newer fund managers might not know about all the ECI and FIRPTA rules. More than once, I've come across real estate fund managers with non-US investors...and without special structuring. This is a double whammy for these unsuspecting GPs.

First, their LPs may need to incur taxes and file tax returns they weren't expecting—this is worse than coal in your stocking. I promise non-US LPs would prefer the coal. In addition, the GP may have tax withholding requirements they weren't satisfying, adding another layer of complexity and freaking out to their operations.

If you're considering accepting offshore capital, please make sure to work with a competent tax lawyer who has experience accommodating non-US investors.

WAIVING FEES TO FUND THE GP COMMITMENT

Now, last but not least: a fancy way to structure your GP compensation that may offer tax and liquidity benefits. We discussed the standard taxation of fees and carry earlier in this chapter. Here, you'll learn about a special mechanism referred to as a "fee waiver" to turbo-charge the tax efficiency of GP compensation. Note that we're going to say "GP" here for simplicity, but technically the fee is often waived by the fund's ManCo.

A cautionary note before we get started. Even when structured carefully, fee waivers are *not* free from tax risk and could be successfully challenged by the IRS given certain grey areas of the tax law. Tread carefully, and work with a competent tax lawyer.

WHAT IS A FEE WAIVER?

A fee waiver is...the waiver of a fee. Typically, the fee being waived is either a fund's asset management fee or an acquisition fee. Basically, the GP foregoes a fee they're otherwise entitled to, and, in exchange, they get additional equity in the fund or syndication.

Fee waivers aim to accomplish two primary tax objectives by "trading" waived fees for something called a "profits interest" for tax purposes:

1. **Defer Taxation:** Defer taxation of fee income. Instead of paying taxes on fee income now, you are taxed later.
2. **Tax Character:** Convert ordinary income from fees into dividends or capital gains taxed at preferential rates.

HOW IS GP COMPENSATION TAXED WITHOUT USING A FEE WAIVER?

On one hand, management fees (and other fees, such as acquisition fees) are normally taxed as ordinary income as the fund pays them (e.g., quarterly after the fund's initial close).

On the other hand, carried interest is taxed at the time it is earned—typically after the fund earns enough income to return capital to LPs (plus potentially a preferred return).

The tax character of the carried interest (i.e., whether it's ordinary income or capital gains) depends on the tax character of the income or gain earned by the fund. For many funds, the carried interest is taxed at lower rates than ordinary income (e.g., capital gains or dividends).

HOW DOES THE FEE WAIVER WORK?

In a typical fee waiver, the GP agrees to *irrevocably* (no takebacks!) waive a portion (or all) of the management fee (or acquisition fee). This election should be made on the initial closing date of the fund or syndication.

In exchange, the GP is treated as having contributed the amount of the fee waived as a "deemed" capital contribution to the fund. In other words, they get a type of equity in the fund intended to be a "profits interest" for US federal income tax purposes.

But...it's not all sunshine and rainbows. There's no free lunch!

THE RISKS AND NITTY GRITTY OF FEE WAIVERS

The GP does *not* get their "deemed" capital contribution (the amount of the waived fee) returned when the other LPs get their capital contributions returned. Instead, they get the deemed contribution amount back on a priority basis from the fund's profits after the return of capital to the LPs. Note that the GP takes a true economic risk here, which is the basis for the "profits interest" tax position. If the fund is not profitable, the GP waives the fee but does *not* get the benefit of the deemed contribution. They waived the fee for nothing (and can't take it back).

After the priority return of the deemed contribution amount to the GP (after the fund is profitable), the GP then receives a return on the deemed contribution as if it were a normal capital contribution. This is in addition to the carried interest they would otherwise earn and any return on the GP's actual cash capital contribution.

Like the carried interest, amounts earned through the fee waiver are taxed based on the characterization of the underlying income generating the return. For a fund like a venture fund, the character is typically long-term capital gains or QSBS, both of which are taxed preferentially compared to ordinary income (as with the carry, special holding-period rules apply).

SHOULD GPS USE FEE WAIVERS?

As you've seen, waiving fees can be a tantalizing proposition. In addition to the exciting tax benefits, waiving fees can help GPs with cash flow. Instead of coming up with a cash GP commitment now, they can use the fee waiver.

However, in addition to the tax risks and the economic risk that the fund might not generate enough profit to earn back the waived fees, there are a few drawbacks to using fee waivers. For example, some LPs might prefer you fund your GP commitment with cash. In addition, the fee waiver mechanism is complex, and your service providers (lawyer, administrator, CPA) might not understand it. Finally, you might actually need the full management/acquisition fees to keep the lights on at the GP.

Congratulations! You made it through an entire chapter on taxes (and, happily, this entire book). You now understand more about investment funds and syndications than many GPs. Certainly enough to get started.

Conclusion

As I mentioned in the introduction, I've gone through much of the fund-building process myself on the GP side. I know it can seem daunting. But now you're armed with the information to make it happen.

WHAT DID YOU LEARN?

Here's a recap of what you've learned:

- **Chapter 1:** It takes about four to six weeks to raise a fund if everyone is on task (including your LPs).
- **Chapter 2:** You'll get paid via carried interest, management fees, and potentially other fees.
- **Chapter 3:** You'll need to build out your team with a lawyer, administrator, CPA, and other professional service providers.
- **Chapter 4:** Your first big decision will be whether to raise a multi-asset fund or a single-asset syndication (many start with syndications and move to funds later).
- **Chapter 5:** Your second big decision will be whether to have an open-end or closed-end fund.

- **Chapter 6:** Once you've determined your basic structure, you'll need to decide on the full slate of business terms and conditions for your fund.
- **Chapter 7:** You'll choose (and understand) a distribution waterfall that's competitive and fair to everyone involved.
- **Chapter 8:** You'll need to work with a lawyer to draft your summary of terms, LPA, sub docs, and (maybe) a PPM to send to investors.
- **Chapter 9:** You may choose to negotiate with investors, in which case you can adjust the LPA or draft a side letter.
- **Chapter 10:** You'll successfully hold an initial closing, signing key documents, and making securities filings.
- **Chapter 11:** You'll call capital and start making investments.
- **Part II:** You'll form and manage your fund in compliance with applicable laws and tax codes. Please note that you'll still want to work with a lawyer, as there's a whole slate of additional laws to consider, including ERISA, CFIUS, and the Corporate Transparency Act.

I hope this all seems much more manageable than when you started this book. If you made it all the way through this book, you'll be miles ahead of your peers (even those who have successfully raised capital).

WHAT'S NEXT?

Now, it's time to make it happen. Re-read Chapter 1, and start crafting your offer. Reach out to friends and family to gauge interest and solicit feedback. Talk to other GPs. When you're ready, start building out your team and preparing for an initial closing.

Good luck!

Glossary

3(c)(1): Investment Company Act exemption for private funds with no more than one hundred investors. See Chapter 13.

3(c)(5)(C): Investment Company Act exemption for funds primarily investing in real estate or real estate–related assets (such as mortgages). See Chapter 13.

3(c)(7): Investment Company Act exemption for private funds that accept only qualified purchasers. See Chapter 13.

506(b): Regulation D exemption allowing private offerings to accredited investors and up to thirty-five non-accredited investors without public solicitation. See Chapter 12.

506(c): Regulation D exemption allowing private offerings with general solicitation to accredited investors. See Chapter 12.

Accredited Investor: An individual or entity who meets certain financial or professional eligibility criteria for participating in

Regulation D securities offerings. This classification has a lower bar than "qualified client" or "qualified purchaser." See Chapter 12.

Acquisition Fee: A fee paid to the GP for acquiring an asset, typically a percentage of the purchase price. See Chapter 2.

Administrator: A service provider that handles certain operations of a fund, like bookkeeping, reporting, and making capital calls. See Chapter 3.

American Waterfall: A distribution method calculating carried interest on a deal-by-deal basis. See Chapter 7.

Auditor: A professional who verifies the accuracy of a fund's financial statements. See Chapter 3.

Blocker: An entity, often structured as a corporation, used to shield certain investors (like non-US persons or tax-exempt entities) from direct exposure to income such as ECI or UBTI. See Chapter 16.

Blue Sky Filings: Regulatory filings required to ensure the legal compliance of securities offerings at the state level. See Chapter 10.

Blue Sky Laws: State regulations governing the offering and sale of securities to protect investors. See Chapter 10.

Capital Call: A request from the GP to LPs to provide their committed capital. See Chapter 11.

Capital Commitment: The total amount an investor agrees to contribute to a fund, typically drawn down over time through capital calls. See Chapter 10.

Capital Contribution: The actual funds paid by an investor into the fund, fulfilling part or all of their capital commitment. See Chapter 10.

Carried Interest: The GP's share of the fund's profits. See Chapter 2.

Cause Event: A specific violation, such as fraud or breach of fiduciary duty, triggering the removal of a key person or general partner as outlined in the fund agreement. See Chapter 6.

Clawback: A provision requiring GPs to return excess carried interest. See Chapter 7.

Closed-End Fund: A fund with a defined term and investment period, commonly used for illiquid assets. See Chapter 5.

Co-Investment: An LP's right to invest alongside the fund in specific deals. See Chapter 6.

Compliance Consultant: An advisor ensuring adherence to regulatory requirements. Especially important to RIAs and ERAs. See Chapter 3.

Continuation Fund: A new fund created to retain and manage select assets beyond the original fund's term. See Chapter 5.

Defaulting Partner: A partner who fails to meet their obligations, such as making a capital contribution, and is subject to certain agreed-upon penalties. See Chapter 11.

Distribution: Payments made in cash or in kind to investors from the fund, often including returns of capital, profits, or other proceeds. See Chapter 7.

Distributions in Kind: Non-cash distributions, such as property or shares, to LPs. See Chapter 7.

Effectively Connected Income (ECI): Income linked to a trade or business within the US, subject to US taxation. See Chapter 16.

Employer Identification Number (EIN): A unique tax ID number assigned to entities by the IRS for tax filing and reporting purposes. See Chapter 8.

European Waterfall: A distribution method where profits are netted across all investments before GPs receive carried interest. See Chapter 7.

Evergreen Fund: An open-end fund designed to operate indefinitely. See Chapter 5.

Exempt Reporting Adviser: An adviser managing private funds under 3(c)(1) or 3(c)(7) exemptions, required to file Part 1A of Form ADV with the SEC or state regulators. See Chapter 14.

Fee Waiver: An agreement whereby a GP waives payment of a fee (e.g., management fee or acquisition fee) in exchange for a "profits interest" in the fund. See Chapter 16.

Feeder Fund: A smaller fund feeding into a larger, master fund. Often important when the fund has non-US or tax-exempt investors. See Chapter 16.

Final Closing Date: The last date on which new LPs can join a closed-end fund. See Chapter 5.

Follow-On Investment: Additional investment in a portfolio company or asset already owned by the fund. See Chapter 6.

Foreign Investment in Real Property Tax Act (FIRPTA): US legislation governing tax on gains from the sale of US real property interests by foreign investors. See Chapter 16.

Form ADV: A form filed with the SEC that provides details about an investment adviser's business, fees, and background. See Chapter 14.

Form D: A notice filed with the SEC by companies to inform the regulator of securities offerings and provide basic details about the offering. See Chapter 10.

Fund: A pool of money collected from LPs and managed by a GP to invest in various assets with the goal of earning a return. See Introduction.

Fund Expenses: Costs incurred by the fund, such as legal fees, diligence costs, and audits. See Chapter 3.

Fundraising Period: The timeframe during which a fund actively seeks commitments from investors before a final closing. See Chapter 5.

Gate: A restriction limiting how much LPs can withdraw in a given period. See Chapter 5.

General Partner (GP): The entity managing the fund, making decisions, and earning carried interest. See Introduction.

GP Catch-Up: A distribution provision allowing the GP to receive their share of profits after LPs get their preferred returns. See Chapter 7.

GP Commitment: The GP's investment in the fund, typically 1–10 percent of total commitments. See Chapter 2.

GP Expenses: Costs incurred by the GP in managing the fund, which may or may not be reimbursable by the fund. See Chapter 2.

GP Removal Clause: Terms under which LPs can remove the GP, with or without cause. See Chapter 6.

Guarantee Fee: A fee paid for personally guaranteeing fund-related debt. See Chapter 2.

Initial Closing Date: The first date on which LPs are formally admitted to the fund. See Chapter 5.

Investment Adviser: An entity providing advice on investments for compensation. See Chapter 14.

Investment Advisers Act: US legislation regulating investment advisers. See Chapter 14.

Investment Company Act: US legislation regulating investment companies. See Chapter 13.

Investment Period: The timeframe during which a fund can make new investments. See Chapter 5.

K-1: A form issued to LPs detailing their share of fund income for tax purposes. See Chapter 16.

Key Person Event: A clause triggered when a designated GP fails to meet their time-commitment obligations and that results in a suspension period prohibiting the fund from making new investments. See Chapter 6.

Key Persons: Individuals identified in the fund agreement whose involvement is critical to the fund's operation. Their departure may trigger specific events or remedies. See Chapter 6.

Late Admission Fee: A fee paid by LPs joining after the initial closing, compensating earlier investors. See Chapter 11.

Limited Partner (LP): Passive investors contributing capital to the fund. See Introduction.

LP Advisory Committee (LPAC): A group of key LPs who advise on fund matters. See Chapter 6.

Limited Partnership Agreement (LPA): The governing document outlining a fund's terms. Applicable if the fund is a limited partnership. See Chapter 8.

Lockup Period: The timeframe during which LPs cannot withdraw their investments. See Chapter 5.

Management Company (ManCo): The operating entity managing the fund's daily activities. See Chapter 2.

Management Fee: Recurring fees paid to the GP or ManCo for fund management services. See Chapter 2.

Management Fee Offset: A reduction in the management fee due to certain events, such as transaction fees received by the manager or costs exceeding predefined caps. See Chapter 2.

Marketing Deck: A presentation used to communicate the fund's investment thesis, terms, and team to potential investors. See Chapter 1.

Master Fund: The main investment vehicle into which feeder funds pool their capital. Often important when the fund has non-US or tax-exempt investors. See Chapter 16.

North American Securities Administrators Association (NASAA): A group of North American securities regulators focused on investor protection and market regulation that oversees tools like the EFD for filing Form D and Blue Sky filings. See Chapter 10.

Open-End Fund: A fund with no fixed term, allowing ongoing investments and withdrawals. See Chapter 5.

Operating Agreement: The governing document outlining a fund's terms. Applicable if the fund is an LLC. See Chapter 8.

Organizational Expenses: Costs associated with establishing the fund, such as legal and accounting fees, are sometimes capped and allocated per the fund agreement. See Chapter 2.

Parallel Fund: An investment vehicle operating alongside the primary fund and investing in the same assets under similar terms, often created for specific investor groups. See Chapter 13.

Placement Agent: A FINRA-licensed broker-dealer who assists in raising capital for a fund. See Chapter 3.

Preferred Return: A baseline return distributed to LPs before sharing profits with GPs. See Chapter 7.

Private Fund Exemption: Regulatory provisions allowing funds to avoid registration with the SEC by meeting specific criteria, such as limited investors or exemption under the Investment Company Act. See Chapter 14.

Private Placement Memorandum (PPM): A document detailing the terms and risks of investing in a fund. See Chapter 8.

Profits Interest: An equity interest other than a capital interest in a partnership or LLC that grants the holder a share of future profits or appreciation in value. See Chapter 16.

Qualified Client (QC): An investor meeting specific criteria under the Investment Advisers Act who is eligible to invest in certain RIA-sponsored funds. This classification has a higher bar than "accredited investor" but a lower bar than "qualified purchaser." See Chapter 15.

Qualified Purchaser (QP): An investor meeting certain criteria under the Investment Company Act who is eligible to invest in 3(c)(7) funds. This classification has a higher bar than "accredited investor" or "qualified client." See Chapter 13.

Registered Investment Adviser (RIA): A person or firm registered to provide investment advice for compensation who is required to file Form ADV detailing their business practices and fees. See Chapter 14.

Regulation D (Reg D): Exemptions under the Securities Act allowing private securities offerings without registration, including Rule 506(b) and Rule 506(c). See Chapter 12.

Secondaries: Shares in a company bought from a third party. See Chapter 14.

Securities Act of 1933 (Securities Act): Legislation requiring issuers to register securities offerings with the SEC unless an exemption applies. See Chapter 12.

Securities and Exchange Commission (SEC): The US agency that regulates investment funds and securities markets and protects investors. See Chapter 12.

Security: A financial instrument, like stocks, bonds, or fund interests, that represents ownership, debt, or a right to share in profits. See Chapter 12.

Soft Commitment: An informal agreement by LPs to invest, pending formal documentation. See Chapter 1.

Special Purpose Vehicle (SPV): A legal entity created for specific investments (often just one asset). Also called a "syndication." See Introduction.

Subscription Agreement (Subscription Documents or Sub Docs): A document through which LPs commit to investing in a fund. See Chapter 8.

Successor Fund: A subsequent fund raised by the GP, often after the current fund's investment period ends. See Chapter 6.

Summary of Terms: A summary of the key terms of a fund provided to potential LPs. See Chapter 8.

Syndication: A legal entity created for specific investments (often just one asset). Also called an "SPV." See Introduction.

Term: The length of time a fund is active, typically including an investment period and a wind-down period before it ends. See Chapter 5.

Transaction Fee: Fees, such as board fees, monitoring fees, or similar, paid to the ManCo (or an affiliate) directly from a portfolio company that may reduce the management fee. See Chapter 2.

Unrelated Business Taxable Income(UBTI): Income generated by tax-exempt entities from activities unrelated to their exempt purpose, subject to taxation. See Chapter 16.

Venture Capital Exemption: A rule that lets venture capital fund managers avoid SEC registration if they follow certain rules. See Chapter 14.

Warehoused Investments: Assets purchased by the GP before the fund's initial closing and intended to be transferred into the fund once it is established. See Chapter 11.

Waterfall: The order in which profits are allocated between LPs and GPs. This is usually under the title of Distributions in the LPA. See Chapter 7.

Acknowledgments

I'd like to give a big "thank you" to the following people, without whom this book would either not exist or be much worse:

- Ekaterina Kachoutina (my lovely wife)
- Alfredo Menchaca Ruiz (TIL)
- Daniel Sepulveda (TIL)
- T. Kyle Bryant (TIL)
- Kareim Oliphant (TIL)
- Chris Schuering (TIL)
- Mark Chait (Scribe Media)
- Katie Lathrop (Scribe Media)
- Eric Jorgenson (Scribe Media)

A special thanks to Adam Krotman, an excellent tax lawyer who co-authored the tantalizing tax chapter. We form tons of funds with Adam. He's the man.

Appendix

Basic Fund Structure

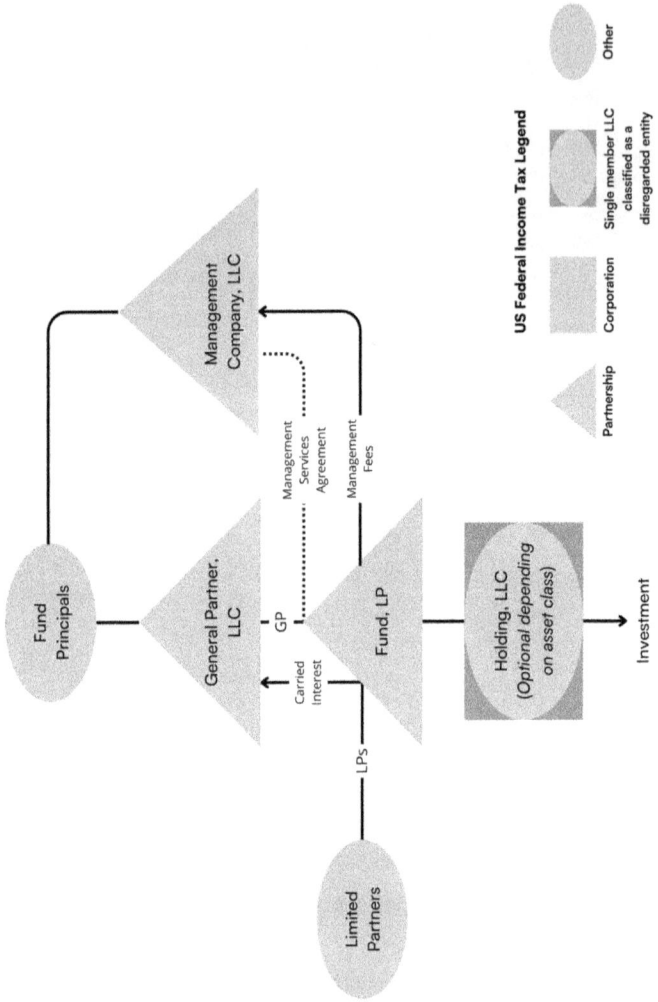

Fund Principals

Management Company, LLC

General Partner, LLC

GP

Management Services Agreement

Management Fees

Carried Interest

Fund, LP

LPs

Limited Partners

Holding, LLC
(Optional depending
on asset class)

Investment

US Federal Income Tax Legend

Partnership

Corporation

Single member LLC
classified as a
disregarded entity

Other

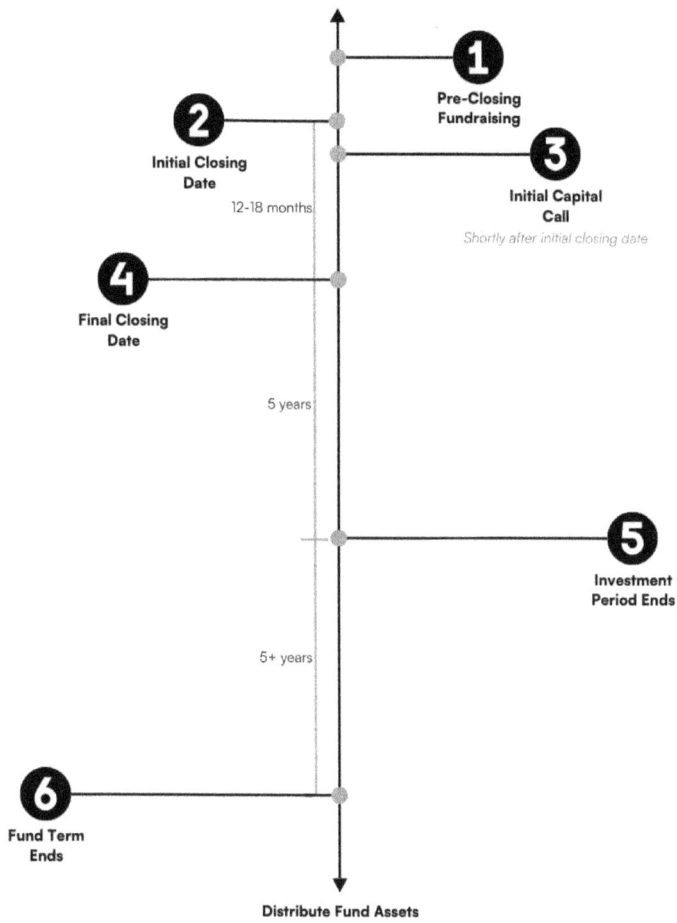

1 Pre-Closing Fundraising

2 Initial Closing Date

3 Initial Capital Call
Shortly after initial closing date

12-18 months

4 Final Closing Date

5 years

5 Investment Period Ends

5+ years

6 Fund Term Ends

Distribute Fund Assets

Simple Waterfall
(One Investment)

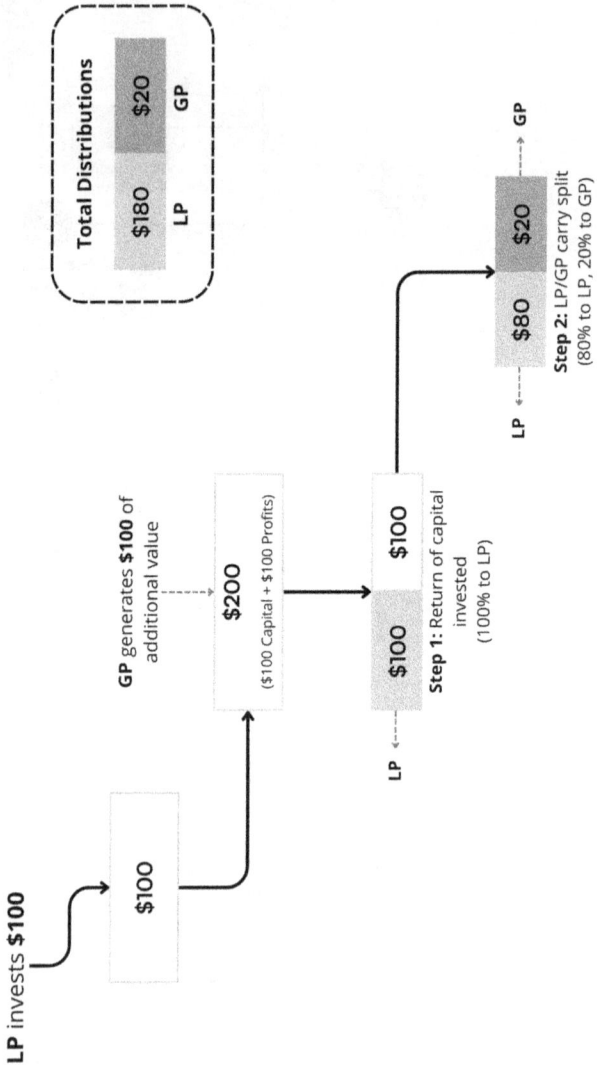

LP invests **$100**

$100

GP generates **$100** of additional value

$200
($100 Capital + $100 Profits)

$100 | $100

Step 1: Return of capital invested
(100% to LP)

$80 | $20

Step 2: LP/GP carry split
(80% to LP, 20% to GP)

LP → GP

Total Distributions

$180 | $20
LP | GP

European Waterfall
(Two Investments)

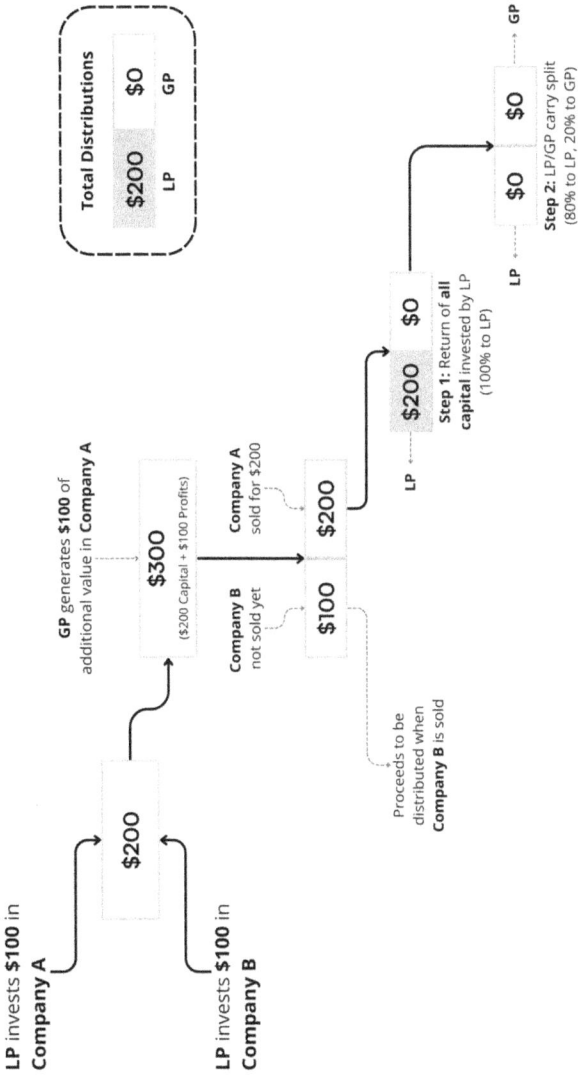

Total Distributions

$200	$0
LP	GP

LP invests **$100** in **Company A**

LP invests **$100** in **Company B**

$200

GP generates **$100** of additional value in **Company A**

$300
($200 Capital + $100 Profits)

Company A sold for $200

Company B not sold yet

$200	$100

Proceeds to be distributed when **Company B** is sold

LP

$200	$0

Step 1: Return of **all capital** invested by LP (100% to LP)

$0	$0
LP	GP

Step 2: LP/GP carry split (80% to LP, 20% to GP)

American Waterfall
(Two Investments)

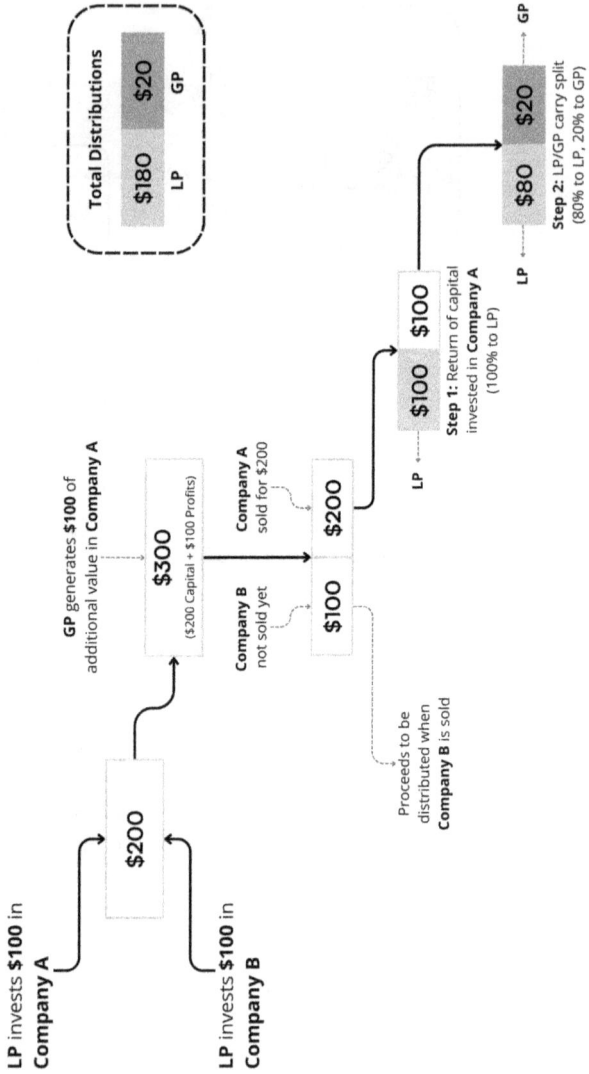

LP invests **$100** in **Company A**

LP invests **$100** in **Company B**

$200

GP generates **$100** of additional value in **Company A**

$300
($200 Capital + $100 Profits)

Company A sold for $200

Company B not sold yet

$100 $200

Proceeds to be distributed when **Company B** is sold

LP $100 $100

Step 1: Return of capital invested in **Company A** (100% to LP)

LP $80 $20 GP

Step 2: LP/GP carry split (80% to LP, 20% to GP)

Total Distributions

$180 $20
LP GP

Waterfall with Preferred Return
(No GP Catch-Up)

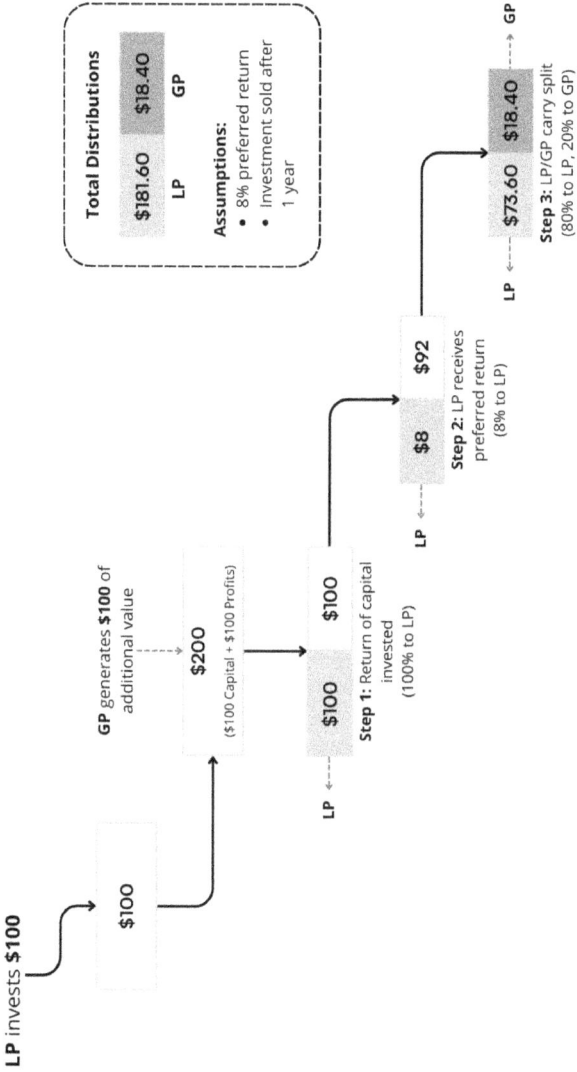

LP invests **$100**

$100

GP generates **$100** of additional value

$200

($100 Capital + $100 Profits)

$100 | $100

Step 1: Return of capital invested (100% to LP)

LP

$8 | $92

Step 2: LP receives preferred return (8% to LP)

LP

$73.60 | $18.40

Step 3: LP/GP carry split (80% to LP, 20% to GP)

LP

GP

Total Distributions

$181.60	$18.40
LP	GP

Assumptions:
- 8% preferred return
- Investment sold after 1 year

Waterfall with Preferred Return
(With GP Catch-Up)

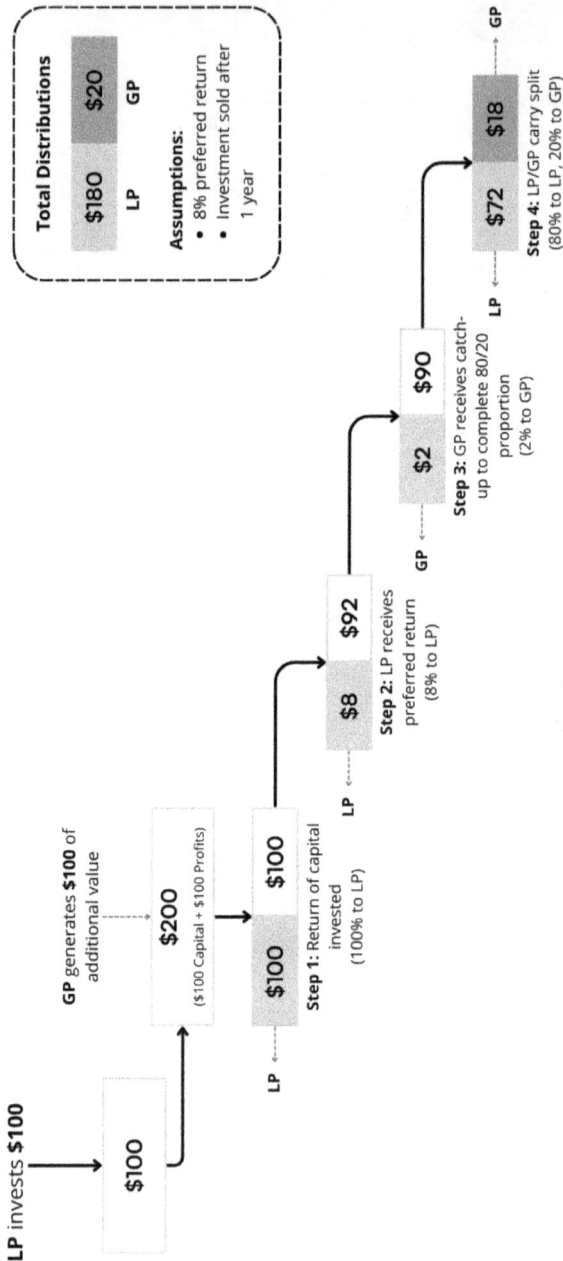

LP invests **$100**

GP generates **$100** of additional value

$100

$200
($100 Capital + $100 Profits)

$100	$100

Step 1: Return of capital invested (100% to LP)

LP ⤍

$8	$92

Step 2: LP receives preferred return (8% to LP)

LP ⤍

$2	$90

Step 3: GP receives catch-up to complete 80/20 proportion (2% to GP)

GP ⤍

$72	$18

Step 4: LP/GP carry split (80% to LP, 20% to GP)

LP ⤍   GP →

Total Distributions

$180	$20
LP	GP

Assumptions:
- 8% preferred return
- Investment sold after 1 year

· 246 ·

www.ingramcontent.com/pod-product-compliance
Lightning Source LLC
Chambersburg PA
CBHW030502210326
41597CB00013B/757